THE FAITH OF A FARMER:
The Ford Reynolds Story

by Derek Levendusky

5 Stones Publishing

INTERNATIONAL LOCALIZATION NET
500 Westover Dr #19552
Sanford, NC 27330

The Faith of a Farmer
ISBN: 978-1-945423-46-8

Book cover: Ron Brancato
Ford Reynolds photo (back cover): Connie Hartle
Derek Levendusky photo (back cover): Caleb Berg

TABLE OF CONTENTS

ACKNOWLEDGMENTS

There are so many people I'd like to thank for helping put this book together. First of all, a big thanks to Randy Johnson and Five Stones Publishing for your excellent service, always with a smile. Your zeal to see the Word of God and stories that glorify Jesus go all over the world is inspiring.

Second, I'd like to thank Michael Tomford, Rick Sinclair, and Tom Wells for the interviews. You helped make this book better and color it with so many details and so much character. Your perspective on the life and ministry of Ford Reynolds were invaluable. Tom Wells, your memory is something of a spiritual gift. I've never met a man more capable of mentally logging names, dates, and details than you. It's remarkable, actually. You've given me gold.

Third, my wife Heid Jo, Ford's daughter, has been a constant source of encouragement throughout the process of writing this book. There have been many days I've been discouraged, not getting to work on the project like I wanted, and she was always there, encouraging me to keep going; to trust in God's sovereign timing for it. Thanks also to my kids Grace, Joye, Essie, Reese, Audrey, and Catfish Jack for the many times over the last decade you let your dad steal a few minutes, a few hours, or a few days here and there to get this done.

I also want to thank GraceLife Church in Avon, New York, and Redeeming Hope in Clarksville, Tennessee. Your constant encouragement in Christ and His gospel have kept the fire burning in my heart to write this book. This is for Jesus, the One who is enough, that others might find Him.

Now let me say thank you Ford and Sarah Reynolds for your great patience and generous grace as I've completed this book. It's taken longer than any of us thought or hoped, but you've trusted God with me to its completion in His good time. I'm grateful for you, for God's grace in your lives, and for the example you've set for your family.

Finally, thank you Jesus Christ for being alive in your Church, demonstrated in the pages that follow. Thank you for the way you love Your people through the work of Your Holy Spirit in the Church. Thank You for the way to love sinners. And thank you for loving this weakling, for putting me in this amazing family, and for the opportunity to write this book.

INTRODUCTION

Some years ago, I felt the prompting of the Holy Spirit to write my father-in-law's biography. As long as I've known him, I've admired his contagious faith, his boyish joy (along with his legendary laugh that everyone knows includes grabbing your belly), and his zeal to see God trusted *for* and glorified *through* divine healing. Of course, the message of his life goes beyond his love of the miracles of God, though this seems to be one of the marks of his calling and a great theme of his life.

My primary motive in writing this book is for my children's sake, that in the years to come, they would know the story of his life, receiving their spiritual inheritance from his excellent life of faith lived with his dear wife, their grandmother, my mother-in-law, Sarah Reynolds.

Second, I believe reading his simple story will inspire many to greater faith; to see the power of the gospel; to eagerly desire greater gifts (1 Corinthians 14:1); to trust God to heal the sick; and to cherish the stories of God's faithfulness contained within. Even as I'm nearing the final draft of this book, a visit back to the farm included a new story of a man healed from prostate cancer. A boyish gleam appeared in my 92-year-old father-in-law's eyes as he told the story.

We are not theological twins, though we don't have to be for me to appreciate his gifts, his passion, his character, his sincere faith, his genuine love, and his fruitful ministry. There is a great deposit of the gospel and of the Spirit of God in this man. My hope is that all tribes of the Body of Christ might read this book and receive from this vessel. For evangelicals, may we be challenged to trust God's Spirit for greater works. For charismatics, may we be challenged by his deep love of the Word and its authority.

One thing I have learned from him is that while one grows old, Jesus can keep the heart fresh and sweet, avoiding the traps of cynicism and bitterness that can mark someone that has "been around the block." Dad never stopped being amazed at the smallest miracle, and has never taken for granted the smallest testimony of how God has blessed him or used him. To this day, his zeal hasn't waned, and I still see tears in his eyes when he speaks of the miracles of God he has seen or heard. All this amazes me. In many ways, I want to be like him.

Of course, I'm also indebted to him for allowing me to marry the baby girl in his family, Heidi Jo. The demonstration of his patience and kindness toward a young, impulsive, conflicted, and sometimes odd young man that would show up at his farm from some 200 miles south was remarkable and gracious. On my first visit, unfamiliar with farm culture, and having driven through an awful snow storm, I kissed the floor on my arrival. This, of course, drew laughter from the Reynolds family, as the very spot I kissed was a high-traffic area for manure-crusted boots several times a day.

Many times, I, or my family, have been the beneficiaries of his gift of healing. I've often been present when he's laid hands on one of my sick children and I can tell you that he prayed with such love and authority that it left an enduring mark on them and their father. He prayed for me when I feared a relapse of malaria, or when I had the flu. He prayed for my wife and children as we've suffered with multiple afflictions. His prayers are always comforting, passionate, and full of child-like faith, like a boy waiting to receive a Christmas gift.

What gifts of the Holy Spirit does he have? Observing the economy of God in his life and ministry, I believe he has the gift of faith, the gift of healing, and the gift of evangelism. Throughout this book, you may see all of these working together in such a harmonious way that their distinction might be imperceptible. No matter how one defines it, his life is full of the fruit of a man who trusts God.

Some of the stories are fantastic and wild. I confirmed what stories I could. He never kept a journal. His journal was in his heart and mind. This book is constructed from interviews with him, along with family and friends.

His reputation around northern New York is that of a highly esteemed man, a man of integrity, a man of principle, a shrewd businessman, a generous man, and a man of great faith. I have several times heard him described as a spiritual pillar in northern New York.

He never had a worldwide ministry, but this story is the demonstration of a man that used his gift in the local church, in his community, and in his region. He is a hero to many; a loved husband, father, grandfather, brother, uncle, friend, and most importantly, son. As you might hope to see as the fruit of the gospel in anyone's life, he seems to be the apple of his heavenly Father's eye and greatly caressed by the Lord.

When I think of him, I can't help but think of the word faithfulness. By intuition the word implies being "full of faith." What we know of the word makes us think that one who embodies such a trait is simply "there." A faithful person is one who is still around after all the hardships, all the battles, all the years. They may not be the flashiest or outwardly impressive. They may not sell the most books or have the biggest church or ministry, but they are still "there." So it is with my father-in-law (and, of course, his wife). He is indeed full of faith, and this has carried him to a long and fruitful journey.

He was not a perfect man. I hope to paint an honest picture of a good man who had strengths and weaknesses like anyone. Though this book is full of stories of the miraculous, he didn't always hit home runs. During the interview for the book, he shared with sadness how he'd recently missed an opportunity to witness to old friends. The door was wide open, but he failed to "make the most of every opportunity" (Colossians 4:5). He freely confesses that God puts "treasure in earthen vessels" and uses weak and foolish things for His own glory. Many of his prayers finish with the assertion, "...and we promise to give you all the glory!" We can also see the grace and mercy of God in Sarah, completing and complementing a man where he might be weak or incomplete.

I must tell you a bit of my own experience in preparing to write this book. As I sat and listened to him share story after story, I found myself freshly challenged to trust God for signs and wonders. I've so often let myself be hindered by my own theological dissents and doubts, but my father-in-law never allowed such entanglements to hinder him. He simply asked God, time after time, for answers to prayer, and never let confusion or adverse results alter his commitment to ask again. After interviewing him, I'm not sure that divine healing is as much about having theological precision on the topic as it is a matter of obedience and action. God said to pray for the sick, and we should evaluate that no more than someone told to walk to the store should micro-analyze walking. You just walk without feeling the need to evaluate your steps. I'm sure analyzing walking would hinder walking and make the journey far less natural. I'm sure one may find a more efficient way to walk or a less productive way to walk. Regardless, we walk. No matter what your gait looks like, silly or deliberate, fast or slow, your walk gets you to your destination. Likewise, we pray for the sick. Jesus told us to do it, so we simply do it, for that is what Christ's followers do.

Many have stopped "walking" (in the area of healing) because of "paralysis by analysis" and have been rendered ineffective. I've been tempted to be among them at times. But in the process of writing this book, I am freshly challenged to simply stop the inner debating and just pray whenever I'm confronted with sicknesses in me, my family, or others. I always remember something Vineyard founder John Wimber said in a church that was wrestling with the questions surrounding divine healing: "We found this out in our church: When we prayed for no one to be healed, no one got healed. But when we started praying for healing, a whole lot more people got healed than when we prayed for no one at all!"

This is not to say that Ford hasn't thought about healing and miracles in light of the Word of God. That's why I dedicated the last chapter of the book to exploring his answers to common questions—especially theological questions—surrounding these matters. But you'll find his answers are all meant to build faith and trust, not win debates.

Ford's daughter, my wife, Heidi Jo, gives a pointed summary of her parents' impact. "So much of Mom and Dad's life has just been investing in people," she explained. "They've really exemplified more than anyone I know the idea of visiting the sick, the widow, and the hurting. They were never afraid to confront people with the gospel or travel to a need in the hope that God might use them."

You will see that in this book.

May the story in these pages inspire you to love and trust Jesus more, eagerly desire greater gifts, and seek the glory of God in the nations, starting in your own community.

Please note: The names of some in the stories contained herein were changed to protect anonymity and privacy.

CHAPTER 1: THE EARLY YEARS

Northern New York has long been a solace from a nervous western world that seems to forget that the best of life is found in the simplicity of nature, family, friends, and faith. Bordering the Adirondacks, the heights of the majestic mountain range known for its pleasant streams and fall foliage seem to ripple into open farmlands and forests across a habitable expanse affectionately called "The North Country." Those who live here seem to own a homeland all their own, far removed from the rush and anxiety of the rest of the western world, with little tolerance for that which is not authentic. In such a place a Ford Reynolds was born and raised, and in such a place a sincere faith was cultivated in him that would bless so many.

He was the youngest of five children raised on Riverside Farm, a pleasant place on a sprawling 265-acres of beautiful farmland bordering the banks of the Oswegatchie River. Born in the farmhouse he would one day own and raise his own family in, Ford Reynolds was the delight of his father James Alfred and his mother Emeline.

First for the Reynolds' clan came Minetta Louise, born in 1922. She would always be called "Weesy" in an affectionate alteration of her middle name. David followed her in 1923, Doris in 1925, Laura in 1927, followed by the baby of the family, little Ford.

Born in 1928, the year Herbert Hoover was elected president of the United States, days on the farm as a boy in the 1930's were filled with hard work, home-cooked meals, and simple living. Richville was a small town of 300, populated by rural townsfolk, farmers, and Welsh immigrants, among whom were young Ford's grandparents. His grandfather on his father's side came from Wales in 1890 and bought Riverside a few years after he arrived.

Those on his mother's side were known to love Christ, and diligently raised their children in church. His mother had a simple, sincere faith, and believed that religious instruction was of the utmost importance for her children. Therefore, she would bring her children weekly to the Baptist Church, which eventually merged with the Congregational and Methodist churches to become the Richville United Church when Ford was nearly a teenager. The only other church in the history of the village was the one that Welsh immigrants established, although it had long since dissolved by the time little Ford came along. The only remnant of that church is the old structure that seems to greet all travelers passing through Richville from the south end, even to the present day, bearing the name "Welsh Society" over the front door. Once a year, a Welsh worship service is still held there.

Ford was a typical boy in a traditional church, disinterested in spiritual things, hating every minute of Sunday School though hind's sight would show him the value of his early instruction. Starting in first grade as a 4-year-old in the little Richville school, he was equally bored with his secular education, doing nothing more than what was required, yet proving to be an adequate, though not exceptional, student. He did play the snare drum in the school marching band, which seemed enormous to the growing boy at the time as it dangled off of his light and lanky frame. Ultimately, young Ford found more pleasure in the cows, the chickens, and the family dog, than in attending school.

His father was a good and honest man, though he was not a man of faith. He rarely attended church (though he had early church attendance to thank for meeting his bride), citing his asthma as the prohibitive factor, but nevertheless he had no problem with his wife and children attending. Even so, as a hard working farmer and the president of the school board, he was well-respected in the community. James had a reputation for being intelligent and wise in money and business (which will surprise no one who knows Ford's financial aptitude), and therefore was trusted with important community decisions like financial matters and the hiring of teachers. He was kind, though not jovial, approaching life, business, and community with a gentle sobriety and sense of duty. In spite of all his responsibilities and work, his love for his son Ford was more than obvious as he would often take the young lad in his lap on cool northern New York evenings to tell him stories of his own childhood on the farm.

The father James also shared a common affliction with his youngest son—asthma—and together he and Ford would inhale the doctor-ordered smoke that was a typical prescription for asthmatics in that day. This would provoke coughing that would, it was thought, help to purge the air passages of obstructive phlegm. Sometimes the poor boy and his father would be up doing treatments in the middle of the night. Little Ford had an awful wheeze at times that would scare his mother, especially when he had a cold. He had one particularly severe episode when he was 7, as a bout of pneumonia was complicated by his asthma and it took him weeks to recover.

Farm life wasn't an affluent one, though his father knew how to make things work. Even in hard times like the Great Depression, James was both thrifty and frugal. He'd borrow money every winter to pay for the grain to feed the cows. Then in spring, when the cows would go out to pasture, they wouldn't have to feed them any grain because the fields provided abundantly, and the animals would produce enough milk to pay off the winter loan. The Reynolds clan wasn't poor, but never knew riches either, nor had any desire to.

Ford's grandfather was always nearby, as he lived in a house just a short walk up the hill behind the farmhouse, and he shared in the ownership and profits of the farm. Sometimes he'd contribute to the workload, like helping "strip" the cows after the milking machines were taken off (getting the last pints of milk by hand), but most of the time was just a welcome presence around the farm. Such was the depth and constancy of family in Ford's life, something that might easily be taken for granted, as life was lived in the context of a stable family and he knew nothing else. The men were simply "there" and Ford never had any reason to think they wouldn't be. When it came time for James to pay his father for his share of the farm profits, he'd send little Ford up the hill with the check, where he would always be rewarded by his grandfather with a smile and a nickel.

Summers in northern New York for the boy were attended by warm days and cool nights, and often included swimming at "the sandbar"—a rare and coveted family-owned stretch of beach on the grassy banks of the Oswegatchie River—along with dozens of local townsfolk on Sunday afternoons. Sometimes Ford would open the gate to the field that accessed the sandbar for visitors, and they'd slip him a nickel or two as well (which he thought was pretty good money). The nickels were adding up for the frugal young farm boy.

Socially, Ford was a bit of a bashful sort, though that didn't limit him in a friendly small town like Richville. Friends abounded, and play time was full of simple pleasures like running through fields, jumping off the barn beam into piles of hay, fishing, or playing games like croquet or stick ball. It didn't take as much to entertain a child in the 1930's as it does in the 21st century. Life itself was simple, with nothing more to make demands on a young lad than work, school, play, and going to bed early. TV eventually came along, but it was not the center of activity, especially since the only available channel was the snowy reception of a Syracuse station. When the family would sit down to view a program, it was considered a special treat.

Usually stick ball games would ensue after school with childhood friends Howard Richie and Gretchen Harmon. Gretchen had a crush on both Howard and Ford, evidenced by her eraser with the initials "HR" on one side and "FR" on the other. Later in life, Howard Richie was drafted into the service in World War II and would eventually marry his childhood friend Gretchen.

As Ford grew, he settled into farm and church life, but with no more spiritual fervor in his teens than he had as a boy. The family Bible seemed more of a house decoration to him than it was spiritual bread, as its content seemed irrelevant outside of its use in Sunday morning services by the preacher. It seemed to him to be a book to ground him in morality, but conjured up no warm affections within his heart to know the Lord. He saw religion as his duty, and doing good as the thing God required of him as well as the basis to, perhaps, be accepted one distant day in heaven. But young Ford Reynolds knew nothing of salvation by grace, neither did he have any hunger to know any more of spiritual things. The clergymen that served at the church he attended did little to wake him out of his spiritual slumber, as some (though certainly not all) brought into the pulpit may have known little of regeneration themselves.

Ford rarely broke the Ten Commandments in any external way, as perhaps religion kept his conscience stimulated and restrained him, and the few attempts he made to do so were met with a terrible guilt. Such a moment was the day he and his friends were up in town playing "kick the can" and noticed a Coke delivery truck parked in a lot, the driver drunk and incoherent. It was such an easy theft! They each nabbed some bottles and ran home to enjoy the stolen goods.

Ford, however, could not enjoy the pop as his guilty conscience tormented him, even to the point of losing sleep, and he expected the police to show up at the door any moment! Even so, he generally lived clean, embodying the old saying that "he didn't smoke, drink, or chew, or go with the girls that do."

The young man certainly carried a sense of obligation to serve his church as he was able, indicated by the fact that he transported the sanctuary organ in his truck once the merger happened, and the Baptist and Congregational Churches alternated the Sunday services between their facilities.

Though later on in life, Ford would have a charismatic experience, the concept of Spirit-filled Christianity was still a strange and distant rumor back in the 1930's. Therefore, the idea of a "Spirit-filled church" was unheard of, as there wasn't a charismatic or Pentecostal church within 300 miles of northern New York. Religion was a simple and predictable exercise of singing hymns, hearing a sermon, and participating in the sacraments. The vibrancy of the Spirit-filled life was not known, encouraged, or perhaps even understood at the time.

Hard work was a way of life on the farm, though his father was always fair and did not drive his sons. Summers days were busy with harvesting hay and oats, and milking, of course, happened year-round. There was always one "hired man" around to help share the load, and he worked for the going wage of $1 a day! Ford would have all the hired men sign his autograph book, a common trend for boys in his day. One man in particular,

Warden Brayton, signed the well-wishing advice, "When you grow old, please be as good of a man as you are a boy."

Young Ford loved playing ping pong (a sport he would later develop rivalries in among his own children), becoming the school champion at one point. He also loved playing basketball. With a lot of practice, he was well known to be a master at "the granny shot," shooting over 90% accuracy as he arced the ball high from between his legs, banking it off the painted square above the rim.

He did just enough, but not more, to pass his school classes. Science bored him, evidenced by getting a 25 on his first attempt at the Regents exam–the state test in New York. He ended up taking the exam several times, and eventually passed with a glorious 65.

Farms are notoriously dangerous environments, and Riverside had its share of scares. The horse teams always provided for adventure. Once, when Ford was at the helm in the wagon, the animals got spooked, and he lost control of one of the reins. The beasts ran maniacally in a circle until the hired man came and calmed them down by grabbing the bridles. In another hairy incident, two yoked horses ran away into the field, choosing to sprint on opposite sides of a tree, ripping the trunk up from the ground as they smashed into it with a violent flash of power.

His father James had another frightening and precarious moment when a wagon full of corn tipped over, covering him under a heap of maize. If it wasn't for the other local farmers on hand helping him bring in the harvest, it may have been his last day. One saw the accident and yelled for help. In a flurry of brute strength only farmers know, the adrenaline-fueled strong-armed men leapt from their tractors and threw off the stalks from the pile until they found their friend. James was fine, but may not have been had they not been there.

Harvest time was a community venture for all farmers, as families would work together to bring in the crops. Until bigger machines came along, community life was essential for success in the fields.

On Riverside Farm, the first milking of the day would happen at 4 a.m. and Ford was usually there. Of course there were days and afternoons, like any child, when Ford wasn't thrilled about milking the cows or shoveling manure, and would claim to have a headache. If his father was aware of his son's bluff, he didn't let on, as he would often spell Ford under such claims or leave his poor big brother Dave to do it all himself! Of course, the boy didn't help his case by playing in the front yard, in plain view of his father, to remedy his unbearable malady. Nevertheless, Ford grew to enjoy working on the farm, and eventually had thoughts of making it his own career as it had been his father's, though this was only one idea among many. With no clear direction, he enrolled in college, and soon he was off to Canton ATC, where he majored in agriculture while continuing to support the family farm.

Dating was rare for Ford in these days, though he and his brother Dave did double-date a few times. On one occasion, Dave was clearly fortunate to find himself with a beautiful young woman as his companion. Ford knew the girl was interested in his big brother and that all Dave had to do was contact her again, which he never did. This baffled his little brother, how he could let someone so "easy on the eyes" slip away! As providence would have it, Dave met his lifelong partner, Dotty, not long after, and his little brother approved of her appearance as well.

It was during this time that Ford was selected to represent Canton College in a speech contest. Being 17 and still bashful, he didn't think he was the best choice but accepted the challenge anyway, not realizing that God was preparing him for ministry. The reluctant young orator won 2nd place in the competition. The one who didn't have a thought in his mind that he would, let alone could, ever preach, was being trained before he was ever converted.

The quiet young man did have some lonely days in college, paying $3 a week to rent a room in someone's home, and he would welcome the opportunity to head back to Richville on weekends to help on the farm and be around family. He didn't have a car at the time, so he would hitchhike the 17 miles down Route 11 back to Riverside. Sometimes he would pay the 45 cents to ride the freight train from Canton to Bigelow, and then hitchhike or walk the final two miles to the property line.

While World War II raged an ocean away and was reaching its climax, young Ford Reynolds was just entering manhood in

1945. Nose to the grind, diligent with his studies, he emerged from the classroom ready to embrace his life and career with a steady stride. He had no aspirations for celebrity or riches, just a blue collar man seeking the joys of a simple farm life.

After his two years at college, it was business as usual concerning religion. Ford continued to attend church, still trying to be a good person, contribute to the community, and serve the parishioners, which of course are all commendable things, but Ford was blind to the fact that these things would not save him. His hope was in his works for his salvation, and he believed God was sure to notice the merit of his noble heart and his noble deeds, and one day reward him. The young man certainly gave mental assent to basic Christian tenets such as the death of Jesus on the cross for his sins and the resurrection of Christ, though there was no witness of the Spirit in his heart, so he remained unmoved by Christian doctrine and had little interest to learn any more theology than what he thought was required.

Entering his 20s, the only difference as far as church was concerned was that his duties increased. First and foremost was the honor of being elected the president of "the prudential committee" which is the governing body of the church. Among his duties was conducting interviews for candidate pastors. In one such interview, he asked the prospect what he believed about the resurrection, to which the candidate answered, "There's no proof that ever happened." Even the unconverted Ford Reynolds had enough sense not to hire such an unconverted minister. He broke the news to the spiritually blind man, surprising him one afternoon as he happened upon the man practicing a fiery sermon in the church office.

Another incident related to these duties was having to tell an eccentric minister that he had been voted out and had to leave. In spite of his termination, the strange man couldn't find another position anywhere because of his excessive behavior, and he remained in Richville, irritating the parishioners with his oddities until the congregation began to dwindle. Ford sought the counsel of the district superintendent, who told him to give the man a deadline for his departure. He did exactly as he was told, and soon the date came and went, yet the strange man remained. When Ford informed the superintendent of what was going on, he came for a visit, but instead of sorting out the situation, he feared the pastor and publicly blamed Ford—for doing exactly what he himself had previously instructed him to do!

This was a deep offense for our young subject, and not long after, reading a common Christian periodical called The Upper Room, Ford came upon the verse where Christ said, "Father, forgive them for they know not what they do." He immediately applied this verse to this situation, forgiving the cowardly superintendent for his betrayal. This shows us how the gospel benefits even the unconverted, restraining from sin and offering principles that, when applied, can bless even the one who knows nothing of true salvation. In the aftermath, the strange pastor found another church and moved away. People slowly returned after he left.

It was this same Scriptural treasure that led Ford through the aforementioned offense that led him through another. There was a certain woman that disliked Ford, and the young man began to forgive her as well and be good to her. He ceased to allow her to control the climate of how he related to her, greeting her and treating her with kindness. At some point in the years afterward, she was saved, and became one of Ford's dear friends. In such ways did the young man learn the power of love and forgiveness.

If one was to be saved by his good works, Ford was certainly a candidate. Beyond all that we've already seen on his resume, he also sang in the choir, fixed the church sewer system, fixed the steeple, and piled up many other commendable works at United Church. As an aside, his hired man helped him on the steeple job—dangerous work high above the ground that made his employee feel important. Not long after, painting this same steeple, this same man nearly fell to his death as the safety rope failed him.

Truly Ford excelled at Christian activity compared to most, always having a hand in things, committed as much as a man could be—and should be—to his religion. He was confident that he would be blessed if he did good. He sincerely believed that he was "serving God" but was unaware that he had "a form of godliness but denied its power." It was his blindness to the fact that these good works did not save him that kept him walking in spiritual darkness. He could not see the light of grace.

Life on the farm kept him busy and even in the mundane, there were always little adventures. One spring day when Ford was in his 20s, he was working with a hired hand cutting off some overhanging branches in the meadow by the river, pushing them into the water with his little John Deere Crawler. Suddenly, the bank gave way and the Crawler plunged into a freefall—Ford along for the ride—down into the river. Thankfully, the tractor didn't roll, or this book might be significantly shorter. Once the moment ended, the tractor was completely submerged and the young farmer had to swim a short way to shore.

His father was away, so he called a company in Potsdam that owned a crane to come and retrieve the machine. They were able to find the drawbar under water, secure a large hook, and hoist it up, swinging it over land to safety. The motor was seized up and would need to be repaired. In those days, the 2-cylinder motor was completely overhauled for $60 and worked for years afterward.

The story of Ben Webb is one that must be mentioned here. In the 1940's, a 16-year-old orphan named Ben Webb took a job at Riverside Farm. Ford's father James gave him room and board, and a little cash for his services. The same age as Ford, they became friends. In fact, Webb was a fixture at the Reynolds' farm and close with the family until 1955. At age 27, one day he left without a word, walking across the field and out of their lives. They never heard from him again and always wondered what happened to him...until one day in 2022, there was a knock at the door. "Hello," said an old man. "I think I used to work here."

It was Webb!

A warm reunion of old friends ensued as Ford and Ben reunited 67 years later. How pleased Webb was to see that the Reynolds still owned the farm!

In the mid-1950's, James inherited his in-law's dairy farm only a few miles up the road from Riverside Farm in Bigelow. Not long after, he sold that farm for $10,000 and bought another nearby property for $9,000 and populated it with dairy cows. He had always desired to set his sons up for success. Farming was in the family. Ford's older brother Dave would one day own that farm and manage it until he retired. Not long after Ford got married (in his mid-30s), his father sold him the family farm, much to his father's delight.

Ford would milk cows and raise a family there for the next 40 years, and even after he retired from farming, he'd live in that house until the day this book was written–the house with the same door Ben Webb would knock on many years later.

As Ford grew older on the farm, his father would say his son was a better dairy man than he'd ever been as the young man excelled in the farm life. His father also said he was married to the cows, as Ford showed little to no interest in marriage even well into his twenties, and he still remained single into his 30's.

That would soon change.

CHAPTER 2: THE MACOMB PRINCESS

Ford's older sister Doris told her eligible younger brother about the Washburn girl from neighboring small town Macomb. She mentioned that she went to Houghton College and that "she's a good-lookin' girl." Ford mustered up the courage to call her and the reply was, "I don't go out with boys I don't know." Sarah Washburn knew *of* Ford, but didn't know him personally. The only connection Ford had to the Macomb princess was his friend Buddy Stammer, who'd married her sister, but even that didn't seem to give him any points. Besides, at thirty-three, Ford was well into adult life, and Sarah was only twenty-two.

Sarah grew up in the Pierce's Corners Wesleyan Church in the Wesleyan tradition. Her father came to a saving knowledge of Christ when little Sarah was only three-years-old, another thread woven by God's sovereign hand into the divine tapestry that would one day give a Ford Reynolds a zealous young woman like Sarah Washburn. One of sixteen children, and very poor, the little girl would often get a ride with her siblings from their pastor down to the simple white chapel that served as the centerpiece of the little town. When they finally got a truck, Sarah and her siblings would load into the truck bed for the journey. Eventually they got a car, though most of the time they'd have to take two trips.

The Washburns were so poor, though none of them knew they were in poverty, that the children usually didn't have shoes until they were of school age, and they had to share coats in the icy cold winters of northern New York. This made church attendance in the winter complicated, as Sarah would have to alternate Sundays with her brother so that they could take turns using the coat.

When Sarah was six-years-old, the kind Reverend Jessmer took the pulpit and remained there for four years. He was a tender-hearted man that took a real interest in the children. He taught the children's Sunday School class and developed a children's choir. His was the first voice that God gave grace to convince little Sarah's heart that she was a sinner and needed a Savior. It was at a simple wooden altar where the young girl knelt and prayed to receive Christ, though she knew little of God's love.

You see, as Sarah grew, the church was also frequented by itinerant evangelists who preached a heavy word of hellfire and brimstone that terrified the child. A sensitive girl, some days she feared being killed before she ever arrived home from the church service. This kind of preaching also caused her to dread the return of Christ, unsure if she would be left behind at the rapture. Such was her spiritual walk until she turned seventeen, and learned something of grace. Just after she graduated, wrestling with her future, an evangelist came to Pierce's Corners and preached on the love of God. It was then that it struck her that God *is* love, that He loved *her*, and that no matter what life brought, whether she be sick or healthy, rich or poor, it would be far better to be with Christ than without Him. And so the proverbial die was cast. She belonged to God. He had her heart, and always would from that day on. Even when evil days came as the years would pass, and she wondered where God was, she never doubted her eternal state. Her assurance never faded.

She also became convinced at this time that God had a plan for her life, and that she must seek Him to discover it. The most spiritual thing to do at the time seemed to be missionary work in Africa, so she assumed it would be her destination. She also thought she may never marry, but considered the possibility that she may be called to serve the Lord alone. After two years at Houghton, where she trained for medical missions, a back injury sustained in a trampoline accident altered her plans, and she found herself back at home, living a mundane life and again unsure of her future. Even so, her zeal to know the Lord and serve him was unwavering. Such was the heart of the young lady that Ford Reynolds asked out on a date. Though she didn't know it yet, it was in God's plans that one day they would marry.

After Sarah turned him down, Ford staked all on his reputation. "Well," he told her in the same original phone conversation, "look me up and see what you can find out about me."

Sarah's mother learned that Ford was pursuing her daughter and was not entirely against the thought, as she'd heard nothing bad about him, knew he was a church-going man, and found his sister Doris to be kind. "The only thing I've ever heard about him that's bad," her mother explained, "is that he has a terrible laugh!"

After Ford gave her some time to discover his quality, he called her again, and this time she was a willing companion. It would be on her birthday. On February 3rd, 1962, he picked her up in his 1959 black Mercury and they went to see the popular new movie *Ben Hur* at the Gouverneur Theater for 33¢ a ticket! Ford, still unconverted though his date had a sincere faith, loved the film, which, of course, is about a man who encounters Christ and learns to forgive.

Sarah found her date uptight and boring, and as an employee at the Gouverneur hospital, checked his hospital records to see how old he was. Discovering he was eleven years older, she thought him too old. Nevertheless, Ford asked the reluctant young lady out again, and she hesitantly agreed. The couple was much more relaxed, and this time Ford kissed his date. He felt like he'd visited a cloud, and that was it for him. His heart belonged to Sarah Washburn. Sarah was equally as lost in euphoria, and it took her some time to return to sanity. Ford would later say that if there was such a thing as an anointed kiss, that was it!

Though Sarah was in love, after some time she realized that her beau wasn't really saved, though she originally had assumed him to be due to his involvement in the church. She was so concerned about this that when the unconverted young man finally asked his sweetheart to marry him, she initially declined, knowing the verse, "Do not be unequally yoked with unbelievers." Disappointed by the refusal of his proposal, he scheduled one last date with her, and that would be the end of their relationship. A sad farewell, he assumed.

Before the final date, Sarah went to her knees. She saw commendable traits in Ford and needed God's wisdom before she denied him. First, she saw a willingness to listen. Even though he knew nothing of biblical salvation, he didn't resist conversing about his soul. Second, Sarah believed he genuinely did not reject God, that he truly believed he was a Christian in his own heart, though in hers she did not believe he was saved. As she prayed, however, she found faith and peace on her knees, believing that God would grant him gospel revelation.

On what Ford thought was their last date, Sarah told her dejected lover, "Well, I got my ring finger measured today." His downcast countenance lifted as his eyes darted into hers. She smiled. He had heard the words correctly. She was accepting his marriage proposal!

That, according to the smitten young man, required another kiss.

Sarah explained to him that she'd prayed and that God had given her perfect peace. What she kept to herself was that she now had supernatural faith that the religious, but unconverted, young man would be born again. Indeed, she knew he was not born again, but believed with all her heart that he was in God's womb, so to speak. She remembered her own religious days, growing up in the church but unconvinced of the true meaning of the gospel until age seventeen. She believed with all her heart that God would do the same for Ford Reynolds, this prince of a man that had come into her life; this kind and handsome farmer that would soon be her husband. She even believed that her beau would one day have a great impact for Christ in northern New York.

They made plans to marry, and this thrilled Ford's parents. Sarah's father was a bit more reluctant because of her fiancé's spiritual condition, though he gave his blessing.

They made their vows on September 29, 1962, eight months after their first date, and just a few weeks before the Cuban Missile Crisis. It was only a week before a group of English boys who called themselves the Beatles released a song called "Love Me Do" in the UK. Two years later, it would hit #1 in the U.S. leading to their appearance on the Ed Sullivan Show watched by 73 million viewers. The culture around them was changing.

The Reynolds' honeymoon was an American adventure. They had no plan but to go south and see where the roads might take them. First, they stopped near Brewerton, New York, just north of Syracuse, and stayed in a small town, run down place called "Eddie's Motel." One might have guessed with such a name that it was not New York's finest—it didn't even have a door on the bathroom! Stops that followed, as they made their way south, included Letchworth State Park in New York, Pennsylvania, Ohio, West Virginia, Maryland, Delaware, New Jersey (where they strolled on the boardwalk in Atlantic City), Washington D.C., and then finally hit their southernmost destination: Horse Cave, Kentucky. Here they stayed in a teepee for $5/night and Sarah journaled, "It was cold and damp but we stayed warm." Gas on the journey was only 29.9 cents a gallon!

It didn't matter where they went. The happy couple was together. It was a long trip spanning some 2700 miles, but all was wonderful. They'd taken $500 with them and this was sufficient to supply all they needed on their 10-day adventure.

Sarah thought her husband would be saved on their honeymoon, and suggested they attend an evangelical church on Sunday to consummate her hope. But it didn't work. It wouldn't happen for nine years.

CHAPTER 3: I NEVER KNEW YOU

Within the first year of marriage, Sarah realized that she and her husband were not on the same page spiritually, and his conversion would not come as quickly or easily as she once thought it would. He simply didn't understand biblical salvation by grace through faith alone, even when it was spelled out for him, nor did he see the need for anyone else to be saved. Sarah's own faith was being tested. She longed to share spiritual things with him, but he could not see.

She had the habit of reading the Bible, which baffled him. He didn't see any need to open the book beyond Sunday morning. Further, when she asked him to attend evangelistic services with her, he flat refused, having no interest at all in them.

Ford knew there was something different about his wife's faith—for starters, she enjoyed church, Bible reading, and religious devotions—but he couldn't put his finger on what it was. Further, no matter what he tried to do to "prove" the quality of his religious merits, his converted wife could see right through it, and he couldn't seem to attain her approval with all his efforts. She tried to explain true salvation many times in many ways, but he was not discerning. She knew her husband was not converted, and that she could not get through to him. She needed divine help.

In Ford's mind, he was a good man, obeyed the Ten Commandments, attended church every Sunday, sang in the choir, and as the reader has seen, was even involved in serving on the prudential committee. Wasn't that enough?

Sarah even had the local minister come to see Ford to discuss his spiritual condition, and her man even fooled him, as the pastor, like a doctor giving his patient a physical, declared him saved! One thing Sarah knew, deep in her heart, was that her husband did not truly know the Lord.

She wasn't spiritually satisfied at the church they were attending, but submitted to her husband anyway. She wanted to visit other churches on Sunday nights, but it always caused dissension.

One day her sorrows overwhelmed her, and she broke down and cried in front of her unconverted husband. Ford also cried and said, unable to discern between what it meant to be religious versus what it meant to be born again, "What do you want me to do? I'm on the committee, I'm preaching Sunday sermons, I'm teaching Sunday School and fixing the steeple! On top of all that, I believe the Bible! Where do I go from here?"

"There's just so much more than what you know!" Sarah explained. "The Bible says, 'You must be born again.'"

"Well then," Ford resigned, "I guess I can't be good enough for you!"

Sarah wrestled deeply with all of this, and privately prayed, "Lord, he's good enough for me. My concern is, is he good enough for You?" It was at this point that Sarah commended her husband's spiritual condition into the Lord's hands, deciding that she'd never again strive with him. She needed God to open his eyes. "He's yours," she told the Father. "You change him, because I just can't do it. If you aren't satisfied with him the way he is, You change him!"

Ford was sincerely happy and confident about his spiritual state. He was sure his wife was mistaken about the condition of his soul, and that he truly had all that he needed. It was simple math: $2 + 2 = 4$. Good works + belief in the Bible = Christian. He didn't understand that, like the unregenerate religious leaders that opposed Christ, you can have the Scriptures without having the gospel. (Though you cannot have the gospel without having the Scriptures.)

Raised to go to church, he believed that faithful attendance was not only a necessary part of his life, but a necessary part of the works required for salvation. Not being able to convince his wife of his right standing before God, and confused about what biblical conversion even was, he resorted to what he knew, and set his nose to the grind of good works he had known his whole life.

His involvement at United Church gave him some sense of spiritual satisfaction. Not that he hungered for God, but church involvement provided the fleshly security of having done enough good to satisfy an unconverted conscience. He even taught Sunday School and preached a few sermons! One of the sermons was directly from a Billy Graham booklet on tithing. "If you don't believe this," he told the congregation, "call Billy Graham!" (Ford himself was not tithing at the time, though he gave more than most.)

Billy Graham was already a star, and his crusades would air on television from time to time, as would evangelist Rex Humbard's crusades. These would stir Ford, but did not wake him from his spiritual slumber. This shows that one can sit under even the most anointed of preaching, and unless grace awakens the soul, one will remain spiritually asleep.

In general, with the exception of his wife, Ford saw most born again Christians as odd, given to fanaticism, and out-of-touch with reality. Such was his opinion of a local man that had been gloriously saved in a Baptist church meeting in Hermon, New York. The man's joy and vibrancy were so much on display that a man of quieter faith like Ford thought him nearly insane. (Ford would be the recipient of similar sentiments when he would one day be saved.) Further, when his own wife would attempt to convince him of the born again experience, he would cite his long list of those who claimed to be born again, and yet would prove the fallacy of their confession with hypocritical behavior. Why would he want to associate with such as these?

A man who claimed to be born again--whom Ford knew well—was known to smoke and drink excessively, and one day he picked up Ford, who was walking along a fence line he'd been working on. When he got into the car, the man said, knowing that his companion abstained from smoking and drinking, "I feel uncomfortable being with you, seeing that I smoke and drink." On another occasion, this same man, when seeing Ford in public, turned the other direction because he had a cigarette in his hand. Remembering these experiences, Ford reasoned, if a "born again" man is feeling guilty around me for my righteousness, what can be so wrong with me?

When it came to the Bible, the young farmer saw it not as a relational book, but a principled one, explaining the basic requirements for living a good life. Surely there is no one who would claim such a life is wicked, as Micah 6:8 seems to describe such a course.

> *"He has told you, O man, what is good; and what does the LORD require of you but to do justice, and to love kindness, and to walk humbly with your God?"* Micah 6:8 (ESV)

And yet, one can attempt to live the life herein described in the Old Testament and fail to see that no one but One has actually done this. One can still be blind to the greater glory of the New Covenant, where God actually indwells his children with His presence, where God is known as an intimate Father, and where the reality of the Holy Spirit is experienced in abundant measures. This resurrected life was one that our religious friend did not know or understand. For all Ford believed about his own simple faith, such passages as the following would confuse him, for he couldn't see the difference between outward religion and inward conversion. He couldn't understand the difference between what he thought *he was doing for God* versus what *God did for him* in the Son. He was blind to justification by faith.

> *"Not everyone who says to me, 'Lord, Lord,' will enter the kingdom of heaven, but the one who does the will of my Father who is in heaven. On that day many will say to me, 'Lord, Lord, did we not prophesy in your name, and cast out demons in your name, and do many mighty works in your name?' And then will I declare to them, 'I never knew you; depart from me, you workers of lawlessness.'"* Matthew 7:21-23 (ESV)

Sarah knew Ford needed a revelation of the gospel, of Christ's sacrifice, of God's love, and of the work of the Holy Spirit in conversion. She continued to pray for him.

Nevertheless, Ford's duties as the president of the prudential committee continued during this season. He'd lead the board meetings, manage finances, and oversee the pulpit committee when the need arose to choose a new minister. Soon, under Ford's leadership, they brought in a good man named Bill Masters who would serve there for many years.

Days turned to months, and months to years. Sarah kept praying, and followed through on her decision to stop striving with her husband, and wait on the Lord.

And the Lord soon had mercy on our poor subject.

In spite of the tension they had about church and the condition of his soul, their marriage was a happy one. By 1966, God had also blessed the Reynolds family with their first two children, Laurie (1963) and Jamie (1964).

Ford was in the barn milking the cows when the call came in that he had a son (in those days, men rarely went into the delivery room). "No kidding!" he shouted with joy. As delighted as he was to have a daughter, his heart was glad with the news of a son, especially since Jamie's birth came only a few weeks after his father James Alfred passed away in November of 1964.

Their first two children would eventually be followed by Jill (1968) and Heidi Jo (1972).

But there was another birth ahead for Ford, the miracle of the new birth. As God does all things "in the fullness of times," the power of grace at work in Ford Reynolds' heart was soon at hand, when his spiritual eyes would open, his spiritual ears would hear, and he would be born from above.

CHAPTER 4: KATHRYN KUHLMAN

One might wonder why it took so long for the Holy Spirit to answer a wife's prayers; to work the miracle of regeneration; to convert the striving young man. These are God's secrets. The Scriptures reference a "fullness of time" for several of God's schemes, and certainly, we could apply this to the conversion of Ford Reynolds.

In 1972, the Watergate Break-In hit the news and Nixon was re-elected after denying any involvement. Meanwhile, Ford and Sarah had their fourth and final child, Heidi Jo, and it was around this time that Sarah's Aunt Edna came one night for a visit. Being a good piano player, she led a sing-along for the family. Before she left, she gave a book to Ford and said, "I want to leave this book with you."

It was *God Can Do It Again*, a testimonial work about the simple and eccentric woman, Kathryn Kuhlman, and many of the miracles she was seeing in her ministry. Edna hadn't even finished reading it, but felt compelled to leave it with Ford. He took it and thumbed through it, deciding instantly that he wouldn't waste his time, though he politely thanked Edna for the gift.

He didn't know it at the time, but God would soon use the book to open his spiritual eyes.

He'd heard of healing evangelist Oral Roberts, but to Ford he was no more than a larger-than-life personality a world away—not much different than a superhero or legend—whose claims of the miraculous seemed so unbelievable that Ford gave the reports little to no regard. Kathryn Kuhlman was easily placed in that same box for our young skeptic. Nevertheless, as an act of courtesy, and maybe slight curiosity, Ford opened the book that night and read the first few pages. He was instantly captivated, and couldn't put it down.

The Holy Spirit was working powerfully. A blind man was starting to see. He soon became aware that he was "born from above" as his heart burst forth with a revelation of Jesus Christ. The spiritual realm crystallized before his spiritual eyes, and all was new. He never could remember the exact moment, but saw it as a birth process, much like a baby is born in the natural with stages of movement toward daylight, so did the man come out of darkness into a marvelous light.

Sarah was delighted at this change in her husband, and rejoiced at the faithfulness of God.

Ford was so captivated by the stories of the supernatural, he rarely read the Bible, but in these days of spiritual infancy read dozens and dozens of testimonial books, including *I Believe in Miracles,* another book about the miracles in Kathryn Kuhlman's ministry in Pittsburgh, PA, and California. Ford wept and wept as he read story after story of God's healing power in so many lives. The wheelchair-bound were rising from their chairs, others received various kinds of healing miracles right in their seats. The teachings of the gospel were plentiful in these works, and he found himself learning Bible doctrine simply from hearing what Kuhlman taught, not to mention the "living epistles" through the stories of God's Spirit at work in many lives.

All of this created a tremendous zeal in Ford's heart for evangelism. Friends and family seemed confused by his enthusiasm for Christ and the gospel. Some were worried about his sanity. The gentle-natured Ford they knew and loved was now bold and preaching Jesus. Attempts to witness to one friend were met with the reply, "You need that, Ford. But I don't." He generally had a gracious attitude toward them, remembering that it was a work of grace that opened his own eyes. Nevertheless, for a time at least, he could sense the concern friends and family seemed to have for him. His siblings remained kind and close, though he lost some friends. Further, many in the congregation at United Church thought him to be one who'd fallen into fanaticism and wanted nothing to do with his aggressive vision to reach the unconverted.

Because of such conservatism, his heart was growing restless at United Church. With all the Lord had done in his life, becoming zealous for evangelism and with the spiritual vitality he now knew, Ford was concerned that there was no evangelistic thrust there. That's when he and Sarah began to entertain the possibility of starting a weekly gathering at their home (without leaving the congregation at United Church). Some mocked him and said, "You'll never get anyone to come. Maybe a few old ladies!" But one night, as Ford was lying in bed, nearly asleep, he heard thunder and lightning and voices in the thunder (he would later find out that such expressions of God's presence were in the Book of Revelation).

He knew in his heart that this experience was from God, and it served as confirmation to start a meeting in his home where he could teach the Bible and pray for revival. Week by week, he sensed himself being trained by the Holy Spirit, growing in his understanding of Scripture, community, and true Christian ministry. The gathering would last for six years with attendance often over twenty people. It became a place where the spiritually hungry would congregate for prayer, worship, and Bible study.

Sarah's Delight

In spite of all the prayers that Sarah had prayed for her husband, she could hardly believe what he had become so quickly, and how deeply the Lord had transformed his heart. To say she was happy would be to fall short of what she was really experiencing. She was simply amazed. Much of what he was learning and experiencing was new to her, too.

She rejoiced daily, and enjoyed every moment as she watched her made-new husband being used by the Lord. Ford was so high on Christ and His savory riches that it turned their marriage into a more blessed union of two saints on a kingdom journey in the same royal carriage. This is not to say that all conflict was eliminated, but all was sweet in their spiritual fellowship, something they had never had before.

Another particular book impacted Ford during this time called *High Adventure* by George Otis. Author Otis shared the testimony of a man that had come to Christ who would become a fine evangelist. He'd attended a gospel meeting and when the preacher gave "the call" to receive Christ, he raised his hand for a brief moment to acknowledge his desire to be saved. Little did anyone know, this small step of faith would grow into a great life of ministry, as the man traveled the world preaching the gospel and establishing Christian radio broadcasts into unreached areas. The author likened conversion to the story of Peter walking on water, reasoning that it was necessary for Peter to step out of the boat before anything miraculous could happen. So was the evangelist-to-be's hand-raising gesture received by the Lord. This was something Ford never forgot and the principle would serve him well in the years of ministry that followed. He would need to take a step of faith toward what he believed to be the will of God if he were to see the works of God in and through his life.

He took such a step during this time to receive the power of the Holy Spirit. A national ministry, known as Full Gospel Businessmen's Fellowship International (Ford and Sarah would affectionately call it “Full Gospel”), began to have a significant presence and impact in northern New York. Several chapters were established across the area, and they had a strong commitment to "the baptism of the Holy Spirit" (Acts 1:8) and evangelism. Ford attended one of their gatherings in Watertown and spoke in tongues when Full Gospel members prayed for him to receive the power of the Holy Spirit. It was like a river of prayer flowed out from him and "every fifth word was 'Jesus'!" The experience was one of the most supernatural that he'd ever had in his life.

When he arrived home, he told Sarah about his experience and she was so intrigued that she demanded, "Let me hear you speak in tongues!" He went into the next room and began to pray so that he might stir his spirit back up and then spoke in tongues with his wife as his audience in the next room. She was amazed and declared, "Wow! That's not you."

Ford laughed with a full heart.

Receiving the power of the Holy Spirit was a significant experience in his life and gave him faith that all the gifts of the Spirit seen in the Book of Acts and in the epistles were indeed for today. He had heard many times that such things had ceased with the closing of the canon of Scripture, but how great was his joy that he was wrong! He found his personal prayer life greatly enlarged and encouraged by this peculiar gift of tongues. He believed that the Holy Spirit prayed *through* him when he prayed in tongues, though he did not understand the language. These prayers, he felt assured by Scripture and the witness of the Spirit, were always in union with the perfect will of God. *What a gift!* his heart rejoiced. *Now I may always pray according to God's will!*

The fruit of speaking in tongues over the years would prove to accomplish exactly what the Scriptures promised for such a gift of grace, that he "edified himself" as the Spirit gave the utterance and was more effective in praying for others. He would never quibble with dissenters over this experience, as he stood with two feet on the ground of biblical affirmation and his own experience. Further, he has many times prayed with others to receive this gift. To the day of writing these words, Ford goes to the church every morning to "pray in the Spirit and with understanding."

This experience of receiving tongues at Full Gospel gave him the faith that perhaps God might give him other gifts of the Spirit, and he was especially encouraged by the generous invitation in 1 Corinthians 14:1, "Pursue love, and earnestly desire the spiritual gifts, especially that you may prophesy" (ESV).

Full Gospel would continue to have an influence in his personal growth and development in ministry as the years went on.

Pittsburgh

During this time, he continued to read books about Kathryn Kuhlman's ministry, along with the many other books he now owned that testified of modern day miracles. The following is an excerpt from Kuhlman's book *I Believe in Miracles,* in Kuhlman's own words:

> *I believe that if the Lord himself would return in person, and do the same works today that He did when He walked this earth in person, He'd have more skeptics than He had when He was here the first time. Back then people did not have as much "worldly knowledge" as they do now. But with the advancement of technology, we have far more tendency to believe in ourselves as the source of all strength, rather than in a God of miracles.*

You see, Jesus said, "Flesh and blood have not revealed this unto you, but my Father which is in heaven." Spiritual things are only spiritually revealed. You cannot force a human being to believe something he does not want to believe. If you do not want to believe in the absolute power of Almighty God, if you do not want to believe that God has the power to heal, if you refuse to believe that diving healing is for today, then even if one were to be raised from the dead before your very eyes you would still not believe.

People are looking for some excuse not to believe. For to believe in miracles means we have to believe in God. And if He is a God of miracles, then we have to obey Him. And we'd rather obey our own sinful instincts than the God who created heaven and earth. So, when faced with a miracle, we prefer to say, "It probably was psychosomatic." Or, "The person was hypnotized."

So, when it comes to skeptics and critics, I leave them with God. But when it comes to answering questions, I answer the questions of the believer and the unbeliever the best that I know how.

Sometimes it is a very difficult thing for me to talk to some inquirer about miracles. He knows nothing about the power of the Holy Spirit, he knows nothing whatsoever about spiritual things. He may be a very wise person and intelligent. But when it comes to spiritual things, he has no idea whatsoever of the working of the Holy Ghost. I try to give answers that I think he will understand.

One day a reporter from St. Petersburg, Florida, who had attended the miracle service in Curtis Hixon Hall in Tampa, came back to my dressing room following the benediction. "I came a skeptic," she said with tears in her eyes, "but I leave a believer."

That's the reason for miracles. Not miracles for miracles' sake, but to lead nonbelievers to faith in—and commitment to—the Lord Jesus Christ.

In one of her meetings, a doctor testified of how God used Kuhlman's ministry with one of his patients: "This woman had multiple sclerosis in an advanced stage. She used to wear two splints and was almost blind. Her abdomen was partially paralyzed. She had a permanent catheter for three years. Three months ago I went with the patient to one of Kathryn Kuhlman's meetings. The patient was healed. Since then she has needed neither splints nor catheter. The paralysis has disappeared. She is now a nurse in the hospital in which she used to be a patient."

Kuhlman, during her ministry and since her death in 1976, has been accused by some of being controversial with her odd way of presenting herself and some of the dramatic manifestations that marked her meetings. But Kuhlman was a simple woman who loved Jesus sincerely. Born into a Baptist family, converted to Christ during a revival in 1921, she never claimed to be a theologian or scholar, but would confess freely that she wasn't. Though she believed the Holy Spirit caused the manifestations that marked her services, she never sought personal glory in them, but only sought to glorify Jesus Christ. She was known for her generosity through her Kathryn Kuhlman Foundation, assisting the poor in Pittsburgh neighborhoods, supporting Pittsburgh charities, funding foreign missions work, and was also a well-known supporter of the Teen Challenge organization, a ministry that works with troubled youth.

One might dislike her emphases, might make her guilty by association, or accuse her of charismania, but it would seem a strain to call such a love-fraught, simple, Christ-exalting vessel a heretic.

Stories from the life and ministry of Oral Roberts also encouraged Ford. One in particular that affected him was the account of a demonized woman that received deliverance at one of Roberts' tent meetings. The story didn't begin so well, however, as the woman actually picked Roberts up and threw him on the ground. Roberts believed in his heart that if he could get his right hand on the woman, she would be delivered, and indeed she was!

Roberts shared another story of how he was exhausted at the end of a meeting, having prayed for hundreds of sick people. Just then, a woman came to him carrying her lame son, his tiny legs hanging limp from her arms. "I'm sorry," Roberts told her, "I'm so tired, I don't have the faith to pray right now. I'm worn right out."

"You pray for him," the mother insisted, but added, "I'll have the faith."

Impressed by the woman's persistence and faith, Roberts mustered the strength to lay his hands on the boy and pray. The next night, the boy came running down the aisle to greet Roberts!

It was hard to find a more inspiring testimony of the power of the Holy Spirit in recent history than was in the life of British evangelist, "Apostle of Faith" Smith Wigglesworth. Ford stood in awe of God's glory in this man's life, a simple man who saw so many miracles that were so stunning that one might be tempted to believe they didn't happen were it not for the multitude of witnesses and books written about him. Even in Wigglesworth's own death, God's power was manifested, as he simply seemed to fall asleep in the arms of a friend.

Stories of the demonized delivered, cancers disappearing, lame children walking, blind eyes opening, and even the riveting accounts of the dead being raised through this eccentric Brit saturated the soul of this new heart, now entering a vista of wonder and worship as he read about such glorious things.

Just as Christ's early disciples marveled at Jesus' authority and said, "Who then is this, that even the wind and the sea obey Him!" So did this modern disciple marvel at such stories of Jesus' power and authority through his humble saints like Kuhlman, Roberts, and Wigglesworth.

These accounts were like salt on Ford's tongue. They left him hungering and thirsting for more of God, more of His word, and more of His power at work in his life.

It wasn't only stories of the miraculous that blessed and taught him, though. As he beheld these "living epistles" he also learned much about God's ways and God's Word through the testimony of their lives. One woman he read about had terrible back problems, and was never healed, yet had a tremendous healing ministry. This taught him that God is sovereign, and that often those He used were wounded healers; that he need not question God or the gift, though he himself may be called, at times, to bear a thorn in the flesh. Wigglesworth had kidney stones, and Kuhlman also suffered physical infirmities in her life, even while she led many to the miraculous waters of God's healing power through Jesus. Kuhlman eventually died under a surgeon's knife from open heart surgery.

Ford was so drawn to the Lord and moved by Kuhlman's life that when an opportunity arose in 1973, he decided to go to Pittsburgh and see this strange woman who burned for God. He was able to join others on a bus that had been chartered from Canada by a woman named Clarice; a woman who herself had been impacted by Kuhlman's ministry. Her grandson had suffered terribly from eczema, which spread all over his arms, and she brought him to Kuhlman's meetings in Pittsburgh. On the way home, the eczema patches began to flake off until his skin was completely clean and as smooth as a baby's. Delighted by the miracle that touched her family, Clarice began to gather as many as she could to go experience the amazing ministry of Kathryn Kuhlman.

Ford's bus arrived at the hotel the night before the meetings began and Clarice led a prayer service in the hotel conference room. During the gathering, another woman gave testimony of how she'd been healed of two different terminal diseases. While she was testifying, Ford had an experience he would never forget. A strange warmth seemed to cover him from head to toe, and when he looked at his hands, beads of water had formed on both. Wondering if this was something everyone was experiencing, Ford glanced around the room, but didn't see anyone else, including the man next to him, who was experiencing the same thing. Wondering what was happening, he thought he might be healing from the asthma that had afflicted him from his childhood. He wouldn't realize until he got home days later, that it was at that time that he received the gift of healing.

The day after the prayer meeting in the hotel, Kuhlman's meetings would begin.

"You'll want to get there early if you want to get a good seat," Ford was told, so he made sure to get to the large, old Presbyterian church plenty early, arriving at 2 a.m. The doors of the church wouldn't open until 8 a.m. Even so, there were already a handful of people there waiting with him, delighted at the prospect of encountering such a great ministry.

By 8 a.m., a line of spiritually-hungry seekers made its way out of the parking lot and down the street. Soon, the atmosphere thundered with the hymn "How Great Thou Art" as the crowd became a choir and the springs of worship opened wide in the open-air. It seemed the whole place was saturated with God's very presence and with an expectation so electrifying, Ford would scarcely see it like that again in the years that followed.

It was all so new. But all so wonderful.

At the same time, the sick and lame were everywhere, all longing to receive a healing. One man convulsed with seizures, others seemed weak and frail from who-knows-what, and still others sat in wheelchairs waiting for the doors to open.

When ushers opened the church, it was like a restrained stampede as people pressed in and pushed their way into the sanctuary. One usher tried unsuccessfully to hold the crowd back. "I came here to get healed," shouted one frightened woman, "and I'm going to be trampled to death!" But no one was seriously hurt.

When Ford finally reached the sanctuary, the faith and spiritual hunger only seemed greater, like divine energy filled the air, connecting all hearts together. They were full capacity in a room that seated 4,000 people. The atmosphere of worship continued until the peculiar and powerful Kathryn Kuhlman took the platform, saying, "My friend the Holy Spirit, the third person of the Trinity, is here among us."

The entire crowd stilled and clung to her every word.

Despite her popularity, Kuhlman made it well-known to her guests and to the media that she had no theological training. What she knew, she was taught of the Lord, and enjoyed a rich relationship with Christ. "How can you live one moment in defeat when you have the great High Priest sitting at the right hand of the Father interceding for you?" she would say. "It's a moment like this that I feel like being seated because you don't need me. It's not me. He is the One."

Often the hearers would experience miracles while listening to her speak or while she prayed publicly. One peculiar practice that became tradition at Kuhlman's meetings was that she wouldn't lay hands on anyone, but still many would be healed and would be ushered out of their seats to the platform to share their testimonies.

Another strange and often controversial occurrence was the common experience of those in her meetings being "slain by the power of the Holy Spirit." Critics would claim she had pushed them down, but she would address her critics while preaching, saying, "It's not true! You'll find people all over this great auditorium who'll be slain by the power of the Holy Ghost far out of my sight with no one touching them whatsoever. I have no healing virtue. I have no healing power. Don't try to reach out and touch me. Don't beg for my touch under any circumstances! Reach up and touch [Jesus]. He's the One!"

While in Pittsburgh the first time, Ford heard many testimonies of healings and miracles.

Later on, he took a second trip to Pittsburgh to see Kuhlman when a Canadian Assembly of God minister decided to take a group. On the way, he told Ford about his first time down, how someone had talked him into going though he'd been somewhat skeptical.

After a transformative experience on that first trip to Pittsburgh, something amazing happened on the way home. The once skeptical minister began to pray for the bus passengers and many fell prostrate by the Holy Spirit's power and were healed. It was for many years that the Lord used this pastor in employing such a ministry. Ford himself invited him twice to local churches in the Richville area with many good results. After the man declined Ford's third invitation, the Holy Spirit spoke to Ford's heart to start his own healing services. Eventually, years later, he would do just that.

First Miracles

Not long after, Ford experienced the first miracle of his own ministry. All of his experiences and witnessing so many wonderful things inspired him to begin trusting the Lord to use him in the same way. The Father, as He always seems to do, started things right in his own home.

Sarah had been having gallbladder issues throughout her adult life, passing stones and enduring infections. One day, Ford's eldest son Jamie came running into the barn, informing his father that "Mom was in pain"—so much pain, in fact, that she couldn't even sit up. Ford was so intoxicated with faith for healing that he didn't even call the doctor, but simply prayed for her. In less than a minute, the pain completely subsided, and she never struggled with it again. Not knowing what the cause of the searing pain had been, she noted as time passed that she no longer had gallbladder problems. She was healed.

A short time later, there was another miracle. An elderly widow that lived nearby used to love to hear Ford sing. For years, he was in the habit of stopping over to visit with her and share songs. When she moved into a nursing home, he stopped by one day and gave her a copy of Kathryn Kuhlman's book *I Believe in Miracles.* A few weeks later, she wrote a letter to Ford, explaining that she'd been having a problem with her eyes that caused them to feel itchy and painful. She said she could still read, but it was very difficult to do so. "When I read the book you gave me about all those wonderful cures," she wrote, "the Lord spoke to me in my ear and said, 'Why don't you ask me to heal your eyes?'" She went on to explain that she prayed and asked God to do it, and that He'd spoken to her heart, "According to your faith, be it unto you." When she woke the next morning, her affliction was gone. "Don't tell anybody at Richville [United Church]," she requested, "because they'll think I'm crazy."

Such experiences confirmed to Ford that he was called by the Lord to lay his hands on the sick and pray for them. He truly believed that at those first visits to Kathryn Kuhlman's meetings in Pittsburgh, he was anointed by the Holy Spirit with the gift of healing. This part of his story would be significant in his thinking in the years that followed whenever he was asked to offer his perspective on divine healing. Though all believers pray for sick friends and loved ones, he was convinced that there is a special gift of healing that only comes through the anointing of the Holy Spirit. This gift increases the power of one's prayers, resulting in more faith and more miracles. This new child of God knew with all his heart that divine healing ministry was part of his portion and purpose. With a happy soul and a boyish faith, he expected great things in the days to come.

One of those great things occurred after it came to Ford's attention that a local well-driller named Larry fell terribly ill and had an 11-hour operation in Syracuse. A mutual friend asked Ford if he would be willing to take the two-and-a-half-hour trek south to pray for the suffering man at the hospital. Ford said he'd be willing to go if Larry wanted him to come. When asked about it, Larry said he'd like that and when Ford arrived, the poor man looked like a zombie. Blessed by the generous act of his coming, he asked Ford, "You really came all the way to see me?" After some conversation about the Scriptures, Larry and his anxious wife gave their lives to Christ. They both seemed to have a sincere faith. Then Ford laid his hands on the man and boldly asked God for a total healing. Soon after, the man was able to return home but still couldn't eat food. Ford went again and prayed and this time God granted the request. He was healed! The very next day, he told his wife, "Honey, I think I could eat a chicken dinner!"

Ford and Sarah were always willing to flow with the creativity of the Holy Spirit, who, like a sailboat on Norwood Lake would sometimes go left and sometimes right. Keeping "in step with the Spirit" (Galatians 5:16) was often part of the story of a miracle. They felt led by the Spirit to move their weekly house meeting to the home of a Richville woman named Cathy who was a dear friend. Her sister, who lived with her, had a growth on her body that made it difficult to lie on her side. After the group laid hands on her and prayed, the growth disappeared.

At this same gathering, Cathy's cancer-stricken daughter also asked for prayer. She was so humble and broken that she got right on her knees in front of the man of faith. The poor soul was frail, weak, and weary. Ford laid his hands on her and prayed, and she was healed instantly! She lived for many years after that.

From those days and onward, his ministry of praying for the sick was almost effortless as Providence afforded him with abundant opportunities to pray for the needy everywhere. Once word got out that Ford Reynolds had a gift of healing, he was called on often to attend those in suffering and offer up prayers on their behalf.

Kuhlman in Ottawa

Within the next two years, Ford and Sarah themselves chartered buses from northern New York to take groups to see

Kuhlman in Ottawa, Canada. In all, they organized three trips and six buses to see this remarkable vessel.

Several significant things happened during this time.

In one of the meetings, Ford was sitting next to a northern New York neighbor, Charlie, who had received Christ at a Kuhlman event in Pittsburgh when Ford had previously brought him along. Now in Ottawa together, Ford turned to his friend and said, "Charlie, look what God can do with a 16-year-old freckle-faced girl that preached 'you must be born again' on street corners." (Ford was referencing Kuhlman's early days.)

No sooner had the words left Ford's mouth, than God spoke the words to his heart with such clarity that he'd never experienced before or since, "And son, look what I've done for you."

And he wept, being moved deeply by God's love.

Ford also saw Kuhlman in Peterboro, Ontario. It was there that she said, "There's someone here that has had long-standing asthma. God wants to heal you now." Ford immediately sensed something happening in his body. An usher could visibly see him reacting, and as was Kuhlman's custom, the usher brought him right up onto the platform. Kuhlman waved her hand toward Ford, and he was overwhelmed with a sense of the presence of God. He would later describe it as an unseen wind blowing over him. He fell to the floor and wept. She said to him, "You will never have it again."

As rich of an experience as it was, Ford would learn a great lesson in healing ministry from this encounter, as his asthma, though much improved over the years, would continue. This would, at times, become a point of frustration and confusion. First of all, Kuhlman seemed to be wrong. Second, he would never receive a complete healing of this affliction. When he wrote to Kuhlman and asked her about it, her simple answer was, "Just keep praying." She obviously had no answers for him, either. Battles with doubt would ensue, but the Lord would ask him every time, "Are you going to believe Me anyway even though you're not healed?" In the years that followed, he began to see this as a tool to humble him, to teach him to trust in the sovereignty of God, and to teach him that all anointed men and women, no matter how powerfully gifted, are imperfect and fallible vessels.

Ford would later learn, in reading the biography of great healing evangelist Smith Wigglesworth, that even he, in spite of the remarkable miracles he saw in his ministry, suffered terribly from kidney stones. As with Ford, this affliction was a tool used to humble him, just as Paul himself wrote: "So to keep me from becoming conceited because of the surpassing greatness of the revelations, a thorn was given me in the flesh, a messenger of Satan to harass me, to keep me from becoming conceited. Three times I pleaded with the Lord about this, that it should leave me. But he said to me, 'My grace is sufficient for you, for my power is made perfect in weakness.' Therefore I will boast all the more gladly of my weaknesses, so that the power of Christ may rest upon me" (2 Corinthians 12-7-9, ESV). Ford would never consider himself a peer of Paul the Apostle, though the effect of the affliction was the same. He would never let his own affliction keep him from praying for the sick, neither would he allow his faith in God to waver.

Sarah's Darkness

Sarah also experienced her own afflictions of the soul, as she would battle anxiety and severe depression. The joys of mothering and the strong affections for children would be accompanied with the dark side of feeling overwhelmed and battling fear for those whom she loved more than herself. God gave grace, though some days were very gloomy. She would learn to cling to God's mercy and strength, and found His power to sustain sufficient. Such verses were proven in her life: *"Because of the LORD's great love we are not consumed, for his compassions never fail. They are new every morning; great is your faithfulness"* (Lamentations 3:22-23, NIV).

One of her first major battles with anxiety came after the birth of the Reynolds' first daughter, Laurie. Sarah was crushed with despair and a sense of inadequacy. Staring at the little girl in her arms the morning after she was born, noting her perfect little features, Sarah found herself sinking into self-loathing, saying, "Look at what she has for a mother!" She worried about the days to come, whether she could raise a child; whether she could successfully mother a teenager—and the baby was not yet 24 hours old! Turning her head away from the child she feared she might eventually fail, the new mother stared into the beautiful northern New York morning sky. The sun shone kindly through the window on her face, while a few pleasant clouds drifted casually along the blue horizon. That was when she saw what looked like the face of Jesus in a cloud staring back at her. It was a generous God to speak to her poor heart in such gentle pictures. She felt nothing overwhelming or euphoric, and heard nothing thunderous or heavenly, save a small still voice in her heart, assuring her that Christ would be with her on this parental journey. Such was the grace that gave her sufficient strength to endure each day when dark days came. She would learn to take her steps one day, and sometimes one moment, at a time.

Ford had a sincere tenderness and compassion toward his wife during these times. Over the years, as these struggles would come and go, she would find in her husband a caring heart.

While pregnant with her last child, Heidi Jo, in 1972, Sarah fell ill with severe colitis. It was so bad that she lost ten pounds within the last few weeks before the delivery date. Facing this illness, the reality of the birth of another child, and all the weight such an event can bring on a young mother's heart, she was overwhelmed. Ford had just been to a Full Gospel meeting and had picked up the book *Prison to Praise* by Merlin Carothers. Moved by the immovable faith, even in suffering, communicated in the book, Ford joyfully told his wife, "Just praise the Lord because you're sick!"

"Praise the Lord because I'm sick?" she retorted. "That's easy for you to say!"

Nevertheless, she read the book, and found her soul comforted by great grace, with a newfound confidence that God was sovereign and in absolute control of all things. Why should she fear? Even when the doctor came into the delivery room, concerned for the position of the baby, manipulating the child's body in preparation for transition, Sarah found herself in a state of peace. Such grace would abide through the entire season of giving birth to Heidi Jo, and the days that followed.

Though Ford prayed for his wife's healing from colitis, it was Sarah's own prayer that God used this time to rescue her from this long affliction. "Lord," she prayed one night, "I have four kids to take care of and I want to nurse this baby, but I can't unless you heal me." It was a moment of intercession like the agony of Hannah praying in front of Eli. The next morning, she woke up and discovered she was healed. At the same time, two other women she knew that had the same condition had to have portions of their colon removed. She was thankful for great, and undeserved, grace.

The children became a source of great blessing and joy for Sarah, especially with the many adorable blunders and anecdotes that would accompany life around the farm for her little ones. When Jamie was only two-years-old, he slowly meandered, like he didn't have a care in the world, to the house from the barn, announcing, "Laurie's s...s...stuck." Mother charged into the barn to find her daughter hysterical, her head stuck in the rungs of a ladder. Apparently Jamie was not called to be a first responder.

Other stories were not so adorable, but were evidence of the faithfulness of God to watch over their children, like the time Jamie was chasing Laurie and she ran recklessly onto the porch, putting her arm right through a glass window in the porch door. Chards of glass lay everywhere—the kind that could sever an artery—yet she had nothing but a scratch right over the main vein in her arm. Such mercies of God were noted and never taken for granted.

In the winter of 1970, Jamie ran after their family dog that had scurried into the field. When Sarah found her son, he was stuck in a snowbank, his boots held fast, while he sat precariously close to a pond covered with thin ice. The dog was on the other side. Had not Jamie's boots stuck in the snow like he'd stepped in hardening cement, he would have pursued his pet to his own peril.

The Conversion of Their Children

One of their great joys was to see the children come to a saving knowledge of Christ. The couple always believed it was essential to pray for the salvation of their own just as they would pray for any unbeliever, as they knew their children were as lost as pagans in a Christless foreign land. The miracle of salvation would be no less necessary, and God wouldn't give a different grace to their children than He would give to the worst lost sinner that comes Christ.

One evening, a Billy Graham crusade was broadcast on television. As was his practice, the old evangelist gave an altar call. During the appeal to respond, eight-year-old Laurie walked over to her father and said, "Dad, I'd like to know for sure that I'm saved."

"OK," her father instructed, "get right on your knees."

She knelt and Ford prayed with his daughter to receive Christ. The next morning, the change was obvious. The miracle of salvation had happened again!

When Jamie was ten-years-old, he jumped up from his seat and went forward to receive Christ in a meeting at the chicken coop after Lonnie Langston preached the gospel. His parents didn't have to say a word to him.

The boy also longed to receive the gift of tongues, but it was slow to come. His best friend received it and poor little Jamie felt even worse, as if he'd been left behind. Then, one night while he slept, he dreamed of receiving the gift of tongues, and in fact, woke up in the middle of the night uttering a spiritual language. How happy he was! His father and mother were amazed to hear the story the next morning.

A few years later, the Reynolds family went to see a Christian movie playing at the Edwards Assembly of God church. It was a movie country singer Johnny Cash had produced about the crucifixion. Though daughter Jill had prayed "the sinner's prayer" previously, it wasn't until that evening that the glory of the cross blazed before the eyes of her heart. She was so moved that she confessed her trust in Christ after the movie ended. She became certain of the promise of salvation and the sufficiency of the cross. It was a revelation that could only come by the Holy Spirit. She never doubted after that.

Such confidence in God's promises was later demonstrated in Junior Church when her teacher, Al Thornton, spoke on receiving the power of the Holy Spirit, followed by prayer for the children. Later on at home, Jill told her mother, "I got baptized in the Holy Spirit today!"

"Oh, you did?" inquired Sarah. "What happened?"

"Well," explained little Jill, "they told me all we had to do was ask and receive, so I asked, and I received!"

"Eventually," her mother encouraged, "God will give you a prayer language."

"Well, I know that!" Jill insisted with a smile. "And this is what I say..."

With that, she began to speak in tongues.

"Where'd that come from?" asked her delighted mother.

"It just came into my head," Jill explained.

Ford and Sarah were thankful for God's generosity to their little girl.

Little seven-year-old Heidi Jo, the baby of the family, was concerned for her salvation one evening after hearing about the return of Christ. She sat on her tender mother's lap and poured out her soul, how she feared that the rest of her family would be taken with the Lord, and she might be left behind. Sarah ministered grace to her daughter, saying, "Well, sweetheart, you believe that Jesus died on the cross for you, don't you?"

"Yes," the teary-eyed, troubled little girl confessed.

"Then that's all you need," her mother explained. Though the child understood in her mind, her heart remained in a state of anxiety over it. She was so concerned, that, when communion was served at Christian Fellowship Center, she did not take it, explaining to her parents, "I can't take communion because I'm not saved!"

"All you have to do is ask Jesus to forgive your sins," her mother explained again, "and ask him to come into your heart."

"I've already done that five times!" confessed the poor girl.

"If you've already done that five times, then that's all you have to do," her mother reassured her. "You can take communion."

She took the elements, but her journey down the dark path of insecurity wasn't finished.

Sometime after, she was in Sunday School class, and her teacher, Bruce LaRose, explained the simple gospel again. When he led the children in a sinner's prayer, Heidi Jo prayed along, and, for the first time, felt assured that the cross had saved her.

Finally, her heart rested.

It is interesting how her heart traveled a similar path, though a shortened version and through a child's eyes, as that of her father, from religious confusion to the born again experience.

New Faces, New Places

There were many of Ford's old friends—primarily Christian friends—who thought his claim that he'd received a gift of healing was strange and unbelievable. Even some among the charismatics doubted that God would want to use him in such a way. One admonished him sternly, when he spoke of the supernatural gifts of the Spirit, "Be realistic, Ford!"

Still holding a lot of authority in United Church, Ford invited an evangelist named Lonnie Langston, a man that had planted another church in the area, to speak. Ford's excitement for hosting his guest waned when only a few from his own congregation attended the special meetings. However, he and Sarah were thrilled to see people come who had never been to church before. Thus the economy of God continued in Ford and Sarah's life, like Elijah in the chronicles of wayward Israel, to reach the Naamans and Zarephath widows outside of church as frequently as those within it.

Ford met Langston after he heard about his special services in a town called Briar Hill. It all began one day when he was working in the barn, and heard a man from Canada named Pastor Belben preaching on the radio. He was sharing about healing, and it stirred Ford so much that he went to hear him in person at an Episcopal church in nearby Ogdensburg. At the meeting, he saw many things he had not seen before. People were lifting their hands and singing loudly in worship; they were passionate, and even sang spontaneously in beautiful melodies between songs. Though he felt a bit awkward and out of place, he was also drawn to their zeal and joy. It was his first encounter with a significant sense of the Holy Spirit's presence in a meeting outside of Kathryn Kuhlman's meetings.

The couple kept going back to those meetings, and eventually heard about Langston's gatherings in Briar Hill, where apparently many supernatural things were happening. Pastor Belben (who eventually planted an Assembly of God church in Ogdensburg out of those original meetings) asked Ford if he'd go check out what was happening at Briar Hill. Even Bill Masters, the pastor at United Church of Richville, after friends of his had attended some Briar Hill services, wanted Ford to check out the meetings, so they went together. The gatherings were held in an old abandoned Presbyterian church.

They weren't prepared for what they would see.

People were falling around the altar in prayer, laying on their backs as if dead or entranced. They would call it "falling under the power" or, as they labeled it in Kathryn Kuhlman meetings, being "slain in the spirit." Other people were speaking in tongues and prophesying; and still others were experiencing extremely dramatic outbursts in response to the preaching and prayer.

Opinions, supportive and skeptical, abounded about these manifestations. Ford could not only sense God's presence at these meetings, but could see the fruit in people's lives who were being touched by it all. Therefore, Ford held his peace, and did not oppose what was happening. Surely he knew that some of it was of the flesh, but also knew God was working deeply in the hearts of others. He knew that the wheat and the tares co-exist in any harvest. Even the Great Awakening is full of stories of the genuine and the counterfeit.

Further, people were getting healed of sicknesses and diseases, and even skeptics would be hesitant to deny that some profound things were happening. One man was healed of heart disease, and still others testified of a variety of miracles, small and large.

It was all so different. But it was all so powerful for our man, Ford Reynolds.

Langston had originally come up from Florida after receiving an invitation from some born again Catholics that had traveled south for the winter and had encountered his ministry there. When he came to New York, he began to host meetings in a home. These were blessed and began to grow, especially when one man received a miraculous healing of his eye. Soon Langston sensed a call from God to continue to preach the gospel to the North Country and moved the meetings to Briar Hill, where Ford went to see this man burn for God in tent revival meetings. The tent that was used for some of those meetings was owned by Watertown pastor Dave Larkin, and it was a young man named

Tom Wells that went along with Lonnie Langston to retrieve it. Wells would eventually loom large in the story of God's work in the North Country and in the life of Ford Reynolds.

Langston was a sharply dressed dark-haired man; young and handsome; a bit heavy though not obese; medium in height though an imposing spiritual presence who commanded an unusual appeal, especially when he would take the microphone to preach. He spoke without notes, often preaching loudly from his heart as verse after verse would just roll out of him with a gifted effortlessness, delighting the hungry seekers in the often-crowded rooms at Briar Hill. This style of preaching was also an unusual experience for Ford, and even Sarah, as both were much more familiar with a calmly delivered, prepared sermon. Yet this style was typical and popular in the heart of the Pentecostal-charismatic movement of the times—"old-time revivalists," they would be called, and Langston was of this ilk. His messages were full of appeals to repent and receive Christ; to live a life of holiness unto the Lord; to welcome the move of the Spirit; and to give one's self for fully devoted service to the kingdom of God. Langston would also play the acoustic guitar, leading some of the favorite charismatic songs of the time.

Well He poured in the oil and the wine
The kind that restoreth my soul
He found me bleeding and dyin' on the Jericho road
And He poured in the oil and the wine!

Drawn to the life of the Spirit that seemed evident in the ministry, it didn't take long for Ford and Sarah to make the decision to faithfully attend Langston's meetings, especially the Saturday night healing service. Langston's ministry found a place in northern New York at the time, a culture marked by apathy and dullness among the religious and the irreligious.

In 1974, the same year Richard Nixon resigned his presidency, God was establishing this new work in Northern New York. Langston began looking for a permanent location for his meetings, and he bought an old chicken house 2.2 miles outside of Ogdensburg on Canton Road. In the years that followed, it would affectionately be called "the Chicken Coop."

For a time, he continued having meetings on Saturday nights, but soon began to hold a Sunday morning service. That was when the Reynolds realized that they had to make a decision: Where would they attend church?

Ford's passion for evangelism was enormous, and he felt compelled to be in an environment where reaching the lost was central to the church's mission. He had hoped that bringing in Langston to minister at United Church would stir a new zeal for reaching the lost, but it didn't have the effect he'd hoped. They were good people with a love for God, but they also had their established ways, traditions, and culture.

For a year, the Reynolds family attended both churches, but with a farm to run, a family to raise, and responsibilities at Langston's church increasing, time and strength were often limited. Then Langston decided it was time to establish a church for the whole family with Sunday School and worship on Sunday mornings.

A big decision had to be made by the Reynolds family.

It came with much pain. First, Ford had attended his hometown church since he was a child. Second, he had many friends there. Third, he still held positions of leadership. Even so, the Holy Spirit was leading the Reynolds family on a new journey. "I want to be where there's an evangelistic thrust," Ford explained to the leadership committee at the church, but they simply didn't, and couldn't, grasp what was happening in his heart.

How could anyone understand what was happening inside of Ford when he himself didn't fully comprehend it? He only knew that the God he had known about all his life was much different than he had ever imagined. And now he wanted to follow that Savior wherever He called him. He wanted to be where Jesus was working—not that He wasn't working in Richville, but Ford had tasted more. He'd felt the power and presence of a living God, had seen Him heal the sick and the weak, and bring lives from darkness to light. He wanted to learn and experience more, and he wanted His family to know this Savior too. He was like Abraham on an unknown journey. This journey would affect his whole household and take him to new places he'd never seen before. It was like the Lord spoke through the prophet Jeremiah.

"Call unto me, and I will answer thee, and shew thee great and mighty things, which thou knowest not." (Jeremiah 33:3, KJV)

So the decision was made. He would leave the church where he'd been since birth, running the aisles in cloth diapers, where he was sprinkled in the practice of infant baptism, where he reluctantly attended Sunday School as a youth and served in many capacities as an adult.

The Reynolds family joined Langston's new church. He and Langston became good friends.

The church would be called Christian Fellowship Center. They incorporated in March of 1974.

CHAPTER 5: THE CFC YEARS

Ford was the first elder installed at Christian Fellowship Center (CFC) to serve alongside Lonnie Langston. Langston actually asked him to serve as an associate pastor, but Ford was content to serve as a lay elder as his cows required his full attention otherwise.

A few other good men were added to the leadership, and the work of the Lord thrived. Saturday evening "miracle services" continued, and it seemed that people were constantly coming to Christ. Miracles were not uncommon. Langston's faith for the supernatural and his gift to gather prospered in this new work, though discouragements were also a companion. Disgruntled and sometimes cruel people were always in the mix, adding more tares to the wheat.

Sometimes an awareness of one's own weaknesses alone is sufficient to make a man stumble into a discouraged disposition. Langston often confided in Ford and once confessed, "You'd be surprised how little I know." He found a friend in the farmer and they were thankful to be on this journey of grace together. The Reynolds also had the joy of watching Langston baptize their two oldest children, Jamie and Laurie, in the Oswegatchie River behind their farmhouse, especially since they'd received the sacrament there, too, many years before.

Friends of friends and relatives of relatives would frequent the early meetings at CFC, often experiencing miracles and salvation. It was a thrilling time. Ford didn't miss a single service. He didn't want to miss anything God was doing. At one point, the Reynolds were also part of launching an outreach service in the basement of a bank in Gouverneur.

There was a lot of "kingdom work" going on in northern New York at that time. Drawn to Langston's work and what God was doing, several key men moved into the area to serve in the ministry. Steve Standish from Elim Fellowship, Jon Benedetti, Bill Norton, and others, moved up from the Rochester area to Ogdensburg because Langston had made a connection with them.

To be a part of the fresh work God was doing, working in the trenches of local church ministry, reached every corner of Ford's heart. The mountaintops of seeing miracles, souls saved, and lives changed were shared with the valleys of watching people broken by sin, division, or suffering. He was often moved to tears.

As an elder he would gain the reputation of being a father to the church, a stable man; credibility incarnated; a conservative man when it came to money. At the same time, he was known as a man of faith. His financial conservatism didn't squelch his optimism for what God might do because he was never afraid to be a realist, to know the hard facts, and in the face of them, to trust a God who *can*. He would gain the trust and confidence of all the people at CFC. The presence of a man like Ford Reynolds and the integration of his spiritual gifts altered the whole trajectory of the church, though he was not the lead pastor.

He was also a man known to pray for the sick. Following in the course of Kuhlman's ministry, Ford sought out, and was sought out, when someone needed a prayer of faith for healing. "He had a real forte for faith and praying for the sick," Pastor Tom Wells would later say. "Those were the earmarks of what he loved and enjoyed. That's the message he embraced and soaked in."

The charismatic movement in those days drew a crowd that was ready to love, laugh, and drink in spiritual experiences. While there were Ogdensburg bars that were frequented like Bob's, Millie's, or Rose's Tavern, the early days of CFC was almost like "Lonnie's Tavern." Many people would actually refer to the gathering as "Lonnie's"—not the church moniker, CFC. Those who came would be well-dressed, like Lonnie was, and most were over 35. The man of God would get up and preach, with great dramatic ebbs and flows, swooning the congregation with his magnetic sway. "It was almost like the Lonnie Show," one would remember. "Not in a bad way, but he was center stage. He wasn't arrogant. He was really seeking God in the way he knew how."

The church had a Saturday night and Sunday morning service, but it was Saturday night that was packed. Sunday services were sparsely attended in the early days.

Meanwhile, Ford continued to milk the cows at Riverside Farm, sensing no call to full-time vocational ministry, satisfied with the eldership role God had given him in the community of believers at CFC.

Soon Benedetti, the young man from downstate, came to serve as associate pastor along with Langston and the elders at the new church. A strong-spirited leader, he was a gifted, seminary-trained teacher with a keen eye for solid doctrine and a fierce zeal for making disciples. Eventually, he took over the Sunday morning service, and Langston led the Saturday evening service. The Sunday gathering grew under Benedetti's leadership, though after a year, he left to work with another ministry back in the Rochester area.

Langston also moved on shortly thereafter, and the elders appointed a young man named Tom Wells from Ogdensburg to be the new lead pastor of CFC. The young man had found faith in Christ while a student in Brockport, NewYork, in 1972 through a local church with Elim connections. He was installed on August 4, 1977. Wells had already been deeply involved in the work in the area, and it was actually he who'd originally brought Langston to the Rochester area, where the preacher would make a connection with the Brockport group Wells was a part of.

It had been a tumultuous transitional time for Wells and the church with Langston moving on, and some did not like the new leadership choice. With opinions and uncertainty swirling in the air, the 24-year-old leader received a call one day.

It was Ford.

"I'm going to stand with you and this church as we move forward," he told Wells. These words were comforting and reassuring to the young man, that this pillar would remain supportive.

One prophetic utterance had dubbed Wells "an unlikely leader" and that might reveal how some may have viewed him in contrast to the much more captivating personality of Langston. The two men were not at all alike and some did not take well to it. In fact, over an 18-month period, much of the congregation left, though the faithful stayed.

Even though his critics were nearby in those days of leadership transition, Wells moved forward in the encouragement the Lord provided. He was truly a gifted and passionate young man, always full of vision, a good word, and had an uncanny ability to mobilize the saints for the work of the ministry.

He'd been working in plurality with Gary Pfeiffer and John Benedetti to serve what was called "Regional Ministry," a relational network that provided care for new churches in certain parts of New York. It had been through his interaction with Regional Ministry that Wells developed a vision for getting involved in northern NewYork, the land of his youth. Within this leadership circle, Wells and the others had great respect for the network's leader, Vernice Smith. He was from western NewYork; a man some might have called "an apostolic leader"; a man who influenced the Regional Ministry men as a spiritual father. Smith had been present in the service where Wells was ordained the pastor of CFC.

Finding the CFC community was, it seemed, a divine appointment for Wells. Desiring the salvation of his parents, he visited northern New York one day to seek out potential churches for them (should they begin to attend one). That's how he found himself at the doorstep of Lonnie Langston. There, a connection was made that led to his involvement in the work Langston was doing, and his involvement with the Regional Ministry group.

Wells grew into the role at CFC, as his college education didn't always lend itself to simplicity in an area dominated by rural folk with a taste for less academic messages. Eventually, he found his groove as his intellectualism was balanced with the understanding befitting of a shepherd who knows his flock. Ford recognized this as a gift of grace, watching the lead pastor and congregation get in rhythm like a band finally performing a song without mistakes. It was one of the many miracles that visited the work of the Lord in those days.

Ford became like a big brother to Wells, nay, even a spiritual father to the young man, helping him with even very practical matters in life. The elder was also known to be good with money, business and buying cars, and Wells learned to lean on his older friend for counsel in these kinds of matters. Though they had the tension one might expect of any close relationship, their union became a strength to CFC for many years. Wells saw Ford as a "class act" and a guiding influence, and credited the older man for the liberty he would feel to be successful in the work. He didn't have the type of spiritual fathering in his background that he would find in the farmer, and would be deeply grateful for it in the years to come. The young leader would find his heart strengthened many times when he would hear his faith-filled older brother say, and with conviction in his voice, "We can do it!"

Reynolds was 48 at the time, twice the age of Wells. Because of the variance in years, the older helped bridge the age gap between the older members of the church and the younger, including with the new pastor. His example taught them, and the young leader, to "let no one look down on you because you are young."

Under Wells' leadership, realizing the chicken coop would not be a suitable facility long-term, the church leaders began to investigate other locations. They looked northward toward Canton, New York.

One of the significant things Wells also did was promote the name "Christian Fellowship Center" more, in a way that moved the culture away from being centered on a big personality like Langston had been. Eight months after he left northern New York, Benedetti returned to minister at CFC, and after observing the culture, told Wells, "The spirit of this place has *totally* changed."

It was during this time, after hosting a prayer meeting in their home for six years, that Ford and Sarah ended this gathering. The negative predictions that it would amount to nothing had been far from accurate, as hundreds had cumulatively met in their home during that season and many wonderful things had happened. Eternity alone will show the fruit of the prayer, the preaching, the discipling, and the fellowship happening in that house on the little farm called Riverside. For a short time, Ford and Sarah hosted another such meeting in the home of a Christian man in Gouverneur. Though this gathering only lasted a short time, it was accompanied by a special charismatic intensity with the manifestation of many gifts, signs, and wonders of the Holy Spirit.

In 1978, the movie Grease hit the theaters. Hollywood continued to drive cultural trends and fashions. The same year, the tragic mass murder-suicide of 909 Americans played out in Jonestown, Guyana, where cult leader Jim Jones demonically deceived scores of people to follow him. Americans were appalled as witness accounts and pictures reached newspapers and magazines, telling the horrible story. Meanwhile, stories of serial killers like Ted Bundy, Richard Chase, John Wayne Gacy, Son of Sam, the Unabomber, and the Hillside Strangler dominated the news.

Fear and darkness gripped the hearts of the western world.

As dark as all of that was, a new light continued to shine brighter in Northern New York. The church was growing and CFC leadership wanted to buy some land and build, and they prayed fervently for wisdom and provision from the Lord for where and how to do it.

Among those on the church council at the time was a man named Don Martin, who served along with George Wells, John Kane, Franklin Ewing (who was a professor at Potsdam), Tom Wells, and of course, Ford Reynolds. One day Martin felt like the Lord spoke to him the number "120" but he didn't know what it meant. He looked it up in the Bible but couldn't make sense of it. He held onto it in his heart, though it didn't seem to bring any wisdom or light as they moved forward, until a profound thing happened. Martin took a map of St. Lawrence County, the largest county in New York, put an X everywhere the leaders of CFC lived, crisscrossing lines between them all, making a center point. Not long after, a piece of property opened up between the towns of Canton and Madrid, right in the spot where the lines crossed on Martin's map. As it turned out, the property was on County Route...120.

Ford, Kane, young Wells, and Grampa Wells drove over to the spot on a snowy February day, with four-foot high drifts everywhere. When the normally financially conservative Reynolds saw the spot, his faith overwhelmed his conservatism. Though he'd normally weigh such a decision, discuss the options, and break down the numbers, it would not be like that today. His heart full, he pointed to the property covered with snow and declared, "That's the spot!" Meaning, "We'll build the church right here!"

With all the circumstances and emotions surrounding the process of acquiring land, it was a moment that would have a significant impact on Well's perspective and faith, and a story he'd remember and recount for years to come. The property was beautiful; a piece of land suited for a stately presentation of a new church to passing cars, while pitching down behind to the Grasse River.

Soon after, Wells scribbled out a simple 100 x 48 design for the church on a piece of paper for Grampa Wells—his grandfather—who gave it to a man named Ron Hurlbut. Hurlbut gave it to a local builder named Joe Tiernan, a man of skill who developed blueprints that became the master plan for Christian Fellowship Center in Madrid.

Ford and Sarah gave a generous gift to this new work, and this inspired others to give. The Reynolds were always willing to invest significantly where they believed God was moving. How blessed they were to see the sanctuary constructed! Though well aware that "the church" is people, and not concrete, wood, and nails, this new facility represented the faith of many, and established a beachhead for spreading the gospel in northern New York for years to come.

The construction of the building was not without adversity. After the initial fundraising campaign, leadership ran out of money for the project and went to a local bank for a loan. There they found resistance to the request for funding, as the facility would be "in the middle of nowhere" and could not, in the institution's estimation, serve for another commercial purpose in the event the church could not follow through on the note. Ford offered to co-sign on the loan, and young Wells called a meeting with the congregation to discuss it. During the meeting, after Pastor Wells explained the situation and possible solution, a young member named Bruce Larose stood up and said to his fellow CFC members, "Wait a minute, this isn't *their* church. This is *our* church. We all need to do our part!"

Grampa Wells, sitting in the back, raised his hand. He had something to say. He stood up and said, "I want to share something. I went out looking for a new Chevy car today and I've already given $1000 to the building fund and I wasn't gonna give any more. But the Lord just rebuked me and said, 'You'd spend $5000 to upgrade your car, but won't you do any more for the building?' So I'm gonna take that money and give it to the church!"

That was like the water that broke the dam. The church entered into a new grace to give to the Lord's work. For the next five weeks, the congregation gave $10,000 a week above and beyond their tithe, and Pastor Wells gladly handed it to the builder to continue the work. It was the most dramatic display of generosity the church had ever seen. Wells would later say that that's what built the Madrid church.

As the church still needed some funding, Wells went alone to secure a note from a bank in Canton. He met with a tall, speculative man whose disposition seemed to have a starting point of skepticism. "I'm not sure this will work," said the man, asking typical questions about numbers, assets, collateral. Then Wells mentioned Ford Reynolds.

The disposition of the man immediately changed. "Uncle Ford!?" he said, a smile suddenly sweeping across his face. "He goes to *your* church? You can have anything you want! If my Uncle Ford signs it I'll give you the bank!"

The congregation moved in on October 8, 1978. Because of an issue with sand in the well water, they couldn't use the heating system on the first day even though it was snowing outside, but they didn't have a care in the world! All was joy. They could see their breath in the sanctuary; they donned their winter coats, but never the mind! They were content as could be in their new home that provided them with a legitimate presence in northern New York.

A young, talented college student from Crane School of Music named Rick Sinclair joined the church during this time—in January of 1980—and he quickly caught the eye of all the leaders. He was a grad student by then, and by September of

1980, Sinclair joined the church staff. He would become the lead pastor when Wells would leave to plant a new work in Massena.

It didn't take long for Sinclair to notice Ford Reynolds functioning in the Body, observing him teaching in Sunday School class, where he would take turns with another member named Ben Klumpenhouwer. He also heard the testimony of how supportive Ford was to Tom Wells during the difficult days of transition from Langston to Wells.

"Ford's support of Tom Wells was a critical part of CFC surviving," Sinclair would later remember. "That was a very hard transition and his support of Tom was very very critical. He saw the gift of God in him."

Stability would be the effect of Reynolds' ministry in the Body and the impact he would have as a leader. Like a seed planted in fertile soil, this trait would bear out in the ministry. By 1982, Wells completed his season at CFC, having led the work during a fruitful season and watching the church mature to a new stability while working alongside Ford and the other men. In the spring of 1982, Sinclair became the lead pastor.

Though Ford saw God's hand on young Sinclair, there had been many changes in the few years since the Reynolds had joined Langston-led Christian Fellowship Center, and as could be expected with anyone, some of it made him uneasy.

That same year, a traveling minister with a prophetic gift came to minister at CFC. He prophesied that though Ford's function was important to the church, he was "never supposed to be an elder." This word was given in front of the entire congregation.

Still young in how to process charismatic things, and with the uneasiness he'd been experiencing, Ford felt compelled to step down, and did so.

This was a difficult and confusing time. He was convinced he was called to be an elder somewhere and he almost left CFC to attend a church in Gouverneur, but it was Sarah who felt strongly that this was not the will of God, and he listened to his wife's counsel. They just needed wisdom with how to move forward at CFC.

Not long after, Vernice Smith came to town, a man who ministered frequently at CFC. He was bringing the Word one

Sunday morning and before the service began, walked over to Ford and said, "I still consider you an elder here. How are you?" This greatly encouraged the farmer.

Soon after, another man with a prophetic gift came to the church. He could move, at times, in swift and clear insight as directed by the Holy Spirit. He'd once been ministering on a college campus and sensed the Lord's favor on his ministry, almost as if God would do whatever he requested. A student asked him, "God can do anything? Well I have a flat tire. Can the Lord fix that?"

"Yes, He sure can."

He prayed and the Lord did it. Jesus was glorified through this strange wonder.

Seeing his old friend's heart troubled, young Pastor Sinclair asked Ford to meet privately with the visiting minister. The man sensed that he should be reinstated as an elder, and Rick was in agreement.

This experience gave Ford and the CFC leadership wisdom in how to handle prophetic utterances. In the years that followed, Pastor Sinclair would take great pains to train the congregation in how to test and apply prophecy, and such efforts were rewarded with encouraging and healthy results.

Ford would receive prophetic utterances with caution, not assuming interpretation without patient consideration, nor accept any undue pressure for self-fulfillment. Further, Ford, Rick, and the leadership at CFC, at no point ever believed in making prophetic utterances equal to or above Scripture. Though the oracles of prophets would *become* Scripture in the Old Testament, they understood that the New Testament dispensation was inferior in the sense that it is "in part" (1 Corinthians 13:9) and subjected to Scripture (1 Corinthians 14:29). Prophecy, then, in the New Testament is welcomed with the understanding of submission to a closed Scriptural canon.

In God's sovereignty, the winding path created a straight one for Ford, who walked out of the experience with a new sense of confidence in his call to serve as an elder. He would stay in that post for many more years at the church.

Ford "abounded in the work of the Lord" at CFC, teaching classes, leading prayer meetings, working through leadership challenges along with the other men who led, all the while investing in anyone and everyone he could in the flow of the Christian life.

Miracles and Healing

Ford didn't always see instant results, or even hear how the Lord might have answered his requests. Some reports of answered prayer would come many days later. On one occasion, he prayed for an older woman from Ontario that was attending Christian Fellowship Center. There was always a steady stream of Canadian visitors that would attend CFC by crossing the bridges in Massena and Ogdensburg. This woman asked for prayer for an unnamed request, and Ford laid hands on her as the Scriptures teach, praying that God would meet her need. It wasn't until two years later that he saw her again. When he did, she told him about the miracle that had transpired in her life.

When she'd originally come to Ford, she had a growth on her foot that had been there for years, bringing pain in every step. On the night he'd prayed for her, the growth fell off and she was completely healed. From that day on, she began to enjoy walks with her husband for the first time in many years. The delighted woman expressed to Ford her gratitude for the kindness of God in granting her request that night two years before.

This testimony, and others like this, convinced him that he would never know all that God had done through his ministry. It was only the goodness of God that allowed him to hear *some* of the testimonies so that his faith might continually be encouraged.

Similarly, he was invited to speak at a Full Gospel Businessmen's Fellowship International ("Full Gospel") meeting in Malone, New York, as a guest speaker. As he was a farmer, he was precisely the kind of speaker they wanted, for Malone was an agricultural area and Full Gospel was known to try to match the speaker to the area's demographics.

This was a new chapter of Full Gospel, and the president was inexperienced in conducting meetings. Unwisely, he'd planned a full-blown lunch along with inviting a music group, all before Ford was set to speak. This created several problems. First, the lunch went longer than normal. Second, as things typically go, the guest musicians were supposed to perform one selection, but the president did not communicate their role properly and they put on an entire concert, including personal testimonies by several band members. It was 4:00 p.m. before Ford was given the platform.

The situation was awkward. Though it all started at noon, his heart was full in spite of the meeting going exceptionally long. Normally, Full Gospel meetings like this were finished by 3pm. Some people had already gone home, and those still present were antsy to leave. Ford had nothing to do but exactly what he'd planned. He shared his testimony, and as was the custom at Full Gospel meetings, he gave an altar call for salvation, healing, and the baptism of the Holy Spirit.

One man came forward, who seemed to be mentally unfit, and when Ford laid hands on him, the man fell to the ground praying, just as he had seen happen in Lonnie Langston meetings and Kathryn Kuhlman services years before. When those who remained saw this manifestation of the Spirit, they began to come forward to Ford for prayer.

One of those who responded was a large man who had one leg that was shorter than the other. In those days, it was not uncommon in Full Gospel for their ministers to pray for those with such a condition, as miracle faith was a staple in their movement. After Ford prayed, he measured the man's legs by holding them out while he sat, and though he did not see a change in length, the man exclaimed, "The pain's gone!" He had been suffering with chronic back pain as a complication from this condition.

When Ford heard these words, he didn't worry about whether or not there was any visible change in the length of the man's legs. Further, he wouldn't be concerned in the days ahead whenever he prayed for the sick whether the prayer was being answered one way or another. God would always hear, he was confident, and was able to touch those whom he prayed for in whatever way He saw fit, regardless of what the one praying saw with his eyes.

Such is an example of the way that Ford would learn from every prayer he prayed. The experience of prayer became as an instructor; a discipler. He would always internalize what God was teaching him, making him a more effective minister of the gospel, and less of an idealist about the way God was working in any given situation. He always carried a strong, almost involuntary awareness of God's sovereignty, that his Lord would do whatever He thought best in response to his prayers. This attitude was not something he simply believed as a tenet of faith, but shaped his whole experience with peace and ease.

This is not to say that he did not pray in faith or ask his hearers to come in faith, as he always sought to build confidence in himself and others when he ministered—that God was generous, able, and welcoming of prayers for divine healing. But when a miracle would not be given, he left it in the hands of his Father as to the reasons and the timing.

On one occasion, he taught a series on healing during Wednesday night services at CFC, a series that lasted a few weeks. During that time, a young woman who attended a local college heard Ford share the story about the man who'd been healed from chronic back pain. It gave her faith to ask for prayer, and Ford laid hands on her and asked for healing. The next day, when she awoke, her pain was gone!

Such miracles reminded Ford that God would not always heal instantaneously. He was good at slow miracles too. God turns water into wine every year through the process of growing and harvesting grapes at wineries, yet no one is amazed at this miracle. But when Jesus turned water into wine at a wedding, all were in amazement. Ford learned to be content and confident that God's grace is just as mighty in slow miracles as it is in fast ones.

Around the same time, Ford and Sarah arrived at Christian Fellowship Center one Sunday morning, and a young woman named Judy, the wife of one of the young adult pastors, ran up to Ford and, bubbling over with joy. Wearing an unrestrained smile, she declared, "The Lord spoke to me in the car on the way over that if you would pray for me, I would be healed of my allergies!"

Ford laughed heartily, impressed by the woman's faith, and would never decline a request to pray when such conditions were presented to him. He and Sarah laid hands on the woman and prayed for her. She was healed in that moment.

During this season, Ford's five-year-old daughter, Jill, fell terribly ill. She was vomiting and her temperature went to 105 degrees. Sarah took her to the emergency room, and her illness was a mystery. They sent her home with medicine but instructed that she should return if the fever didn't wane. The next day, it was the same, so she was hospitalized. In spite of IVs and medicines, they could not bring the fever down, and they remained mystified by her condition. When the following morning brought the same news, Ford went in and prayed for her while Sarah stayed home with the children. He came home with grim news. "You better get back to the hospital quickly," he said, "she isn't getting any better."

On the way to the hospital, her mother's heart burdened and broken, Sarah wept. She knew her child was in grave danger. Such a condition put little Jill face to face with the possibility of brain damage, not to mention death. "Lord," her frightened mother cried out, "my daughter is in Your hands! It's all up to You! I surrender to Your will. But if there's any way that You can accomplish Your purposes while keeping her healthy, please have mercy on us and give us back our child. Yet not my will but Yours be done!"

When she arrived at the hospital, her daughter's temperature was already starting to drop and she'd even requested food. Though the doctor was skeptical, Sarah said, "Doctor, I think she's better."

Sure enough, she was recovering. The doctors never did know what was wrong with the poor child.

Ford and Sarah thanked God for what they considered a great miracle.

There were many reasons to thank the Giver of all good gifts during their days at CFC. Barren women had children, bodies were healed, diseases cured, families restored, lives changed. The laws of sowing and reaping were active in Northern New York and they were good days—sow bountifully, reap bountifully. Pray a lot, get lots of answers. This isn't to imply that everyone got healed anytime they prayed, but their attitude continued to follow the John Wimber principle: More people get healed when we pray for the sick than when we don't pray at all.

One man that always encouraged Ford's faith and expectation for divine healing was Tom Wells' grandfather, a man affectionately called "Grampa" Wells. He was an older man, like Ford, and had contagious faith, owning an inspiring recklessness that even shocked his understudy at times. It was such faith that emboldened Ford even more to use his gift and employ his own faith.

Grampa Wells and Ford would often team together, like the time they were ministering at the altar at CFC one Sunday morning. A Catholic man came forward and told them that his arm had been broken in two places, and that he was in a lot of pain. When they asked him if he had trusted in Jesus for salvation and been born again, he confessed that he was not sure about the state of his soul. They prayed with him to be saved, and then prayed for his arm to be healed. The pain left instantly! The man beamed with joy for blessings temporal and eternal.

Grampa Wells

Ford met Albert "Grampa" Wells in the early days of the chicken coop. He was the grandfather of Tom Wells, and eventually came to Christ as a result of his grandson's witness when the newly-saved young man shared his faith with his whole family.

The circumstances of his moment of salvation were dramatic. His wife had a severe head injury, and the prognosis discouraged Grampa Wells so severely that he planned his own suicide—he would drive to the Ogdensburg Bridge and jump to his death. While on his way to his dark destination, he later testified, God jerked his car to the side of the road. There he had a personal visitation with the presence of God that altered not only the course of his car, but the course of his life. It was the same God who interrupted the plans of Saul of Tarsus on the road to Damascus. Now he had interrupted Albert of Ogdensburg.

Grampa Wells returned home and began to pray in faith for his wife, joining the prayers of his grandson, and she was healed of her injury, rescued from the otherwise hopeless path she was on. The same might be said for the man that had been under the dark cloud of depression.

It was a new birth for the 68-year-old man. He was born into God's family and the entire trajectory of his life would never be the same.

Even before his conversion, he himself was healed of a heart condition. And once the Light broke into his soul, he would never be the same, burning with holy passion for Jesus and lost souls.

For a long time, he prayed for a healing ministry. God gave him the desire of his heart and also gave him the gift of faith. He had a remarkable boyish ability to believe God for things no one else dared to ask for. There were times when he just knew that someone would be healed. He once told a blind man, "You're going to be slain in the spirit, and your eyes are going to be healed." And it happened.

He and Ford were very close, and Grampa Wells often told him that he trusted him like a son, for he was over 20 years older than Ford. He was indeed a good friend, and always seemed to appreciate Ford and his ministry. Reynolds was never more certain of a man's confidence in him and his calling than when he was around Grampa Wells, who built him up and encouraged him often. They were partners in ministry more than once, serving as a team of two like Christ would send out his early disciples. They would minister together at Full Gospel meetings, church meetings, and in home visitations. Indeed the two became like the fathers of the church. Everyone respected them. If you needed prayer, you wanted Grampa Wells and Ford Reynolds to pray for you.

A simple man, Wells had a bicycle shop in Ogdensburg; a small city on the banks of the St. Lawrence River—a great river that separated the United States from Canada. It was not uncommon for him to share Christ with a customer or pray for someone's need in that shop. He also held frequent prayer meetings there, often attended by believers from CFC and other area churches. A gentle man, he had a smile that made you feel like he was your own grandfather; a warmth that exuded love and made one immediately feel like they mattered.

The mark of his life, however, much like his friend Ford, was faith for divine healing. He was a product of the Pentecostal movement that imparted great faith to its adherents. Langston had a significant impact on the man, and there was an ease about the connection between the two as both longed for revival and the miraculous.

Wells would go to the hospital almost every day, asking the Holy Spirit for guidance as to which rooms to visit, often laying hands on the sick. Miracles were frequent and sometimes astonishing.

He believed that Jesus Christ had *now power*. Certainly we will all be ultimately healed in heaven, but Grampa Wells would not neglect Christ's "now power" to heal as well. Just as Martha confessed when Jesus told her that Lazarus would rise, "I know that he will rise again in the resurrection on the last day." Jesus said, "I am the resurrection and the life." She was right, but what she didn't know was that Jesus was going to do it *now*. Such was the shocking nature of Grampa Well's faith.

The Reynolds children would later remember the many times the dear old man would come to their door, requesting the company of their father on one of his many hospital adventures, a divine errand for no other purpose than to pray for the weak as the Spirit gave opportunity. Ford and Grampa Wells found courage and strength in one another's company as they went out on missions of mercy.

Grampa Wells once went into a room, led by the Holy Spirit, and felt impressed to pray for a man lying in a bed on his side. He was dying. In obedience to the Holy Spirit, Wells prayed for the man. When he returned a few days later, the man was gone, and Wells thought he might have passed. Inquiring about him, he found out that the man had been completely healed and had already gone home!

Another miraculous story was repeated often throughout the years at Christian Fellowship Center.

Grampa Wells' son George (Pastor Tom Wells' father) had cancer, and one of his ribs was eaten away. The doctor told him he only had six months to live. Ford and Grampa Wells, along with the elders at CFC, laid hands on him and asked God to heal him. The poor man was weak and ashen in color, preparing to die. After they prayed, the cancer-stricken man said, "Well, we'll see what the Lord does."

He went off to Florida and not long after he arrived, remarked to his wife, "It really is nice down here." He himself couldn't help but notice how good he felt. His condition seemed to steadily improve during his time in the kind Florida sun, and soon he returned back to northern New York, where he continued to feel strong.

He decided to get an X-ray.

The rib was not only healed and rid of all cancer, but had grown back.

O how this built up the faith of everyone who heard the story!

Grampa Wells prayed that one day he might die in his sleep, and the Lord granted him his desire at the age of 80. Ford was asked to eulogize his dear old friend, and for a very rare moment in his life, was so overcome with tears he could not speak. Grampa Wells' faith had served as an example and inspiration to Ford, and in the years to come, his memory would embolden his one-time partner in ministry many times.

Reynolds never had a chance to pray that the dead might be raised, though Grampa Wells asked the Lord if he might raise the dead. He never saw his prayer answered, at least in the way he had hoped, though he did receive an answer from the Lord.

Wells was once asked to come pray over a man that had passed away, and he thought it might be the moment that his prayer would be answered. As he prayed, the cold, dead corpse grew warm as if life were returning to it. The man, however, did not ultimately revive. Wells concluded that God had, in his kindness, showed His zealous son that He had heard his prayer, but also that it was not His will that he should partake in such a miracle.

Ford and Grampa Wells became like Peter and John, serving together in the church and community. You could always find them at the altar during church services praying for anyone who would come with any need.

During these days, CFC hosted a viewing of the movie "The Cross and the Switchblade"—the famous conversion story of David Wilkerson. A man came to see the film who afterward came forward to receive Christ. Grampa Wells and Ford were on the ministry team at the altar, and they prayed with him as he came to faith. Afterward, the man asked if they would pray for him to be healed, explaining that he'd broken his arm in three different places and had constant pain for years. The twosome asked God to heal him and the pain left his arm immediately. It was a miracle, though they never saw the man again—another seed sown in God's great harvest field.

Just as Jesus sent them out in two's, it seemed for this season that the Lord had put Wells and Reynolds together for His glorious assignments. They fed off one another's faith and encouragement until the day the older man passed away, leaving behind a legacy of faith and love.

His Singing

Ford was known to have a booming singing voice, one that would stand out, especially when the congregation would sing hymns. He loved to worship, and was unashamed at lifting his hands and his voice to express his deep love for God. Though not vocationally (until his daughter Heidi started a singing career with her husband), singing was always in the family. His grandfather (on his father's side) was called "Lupsh" and used to frequently lend his vocal talent to the Welsh Church in Richville. Ford never had any idea where such a peculiar nickname originated.

Tom Wells, who had no special affinity for hymns as he cut his musical teeth on classic rock music before he came to Christ in college, found Ford's singing voice to be deeply moving. When he'd sing songs like "It Is Well," he would say it was like the song went right through you—through your heart, through your spirit.

It was during these CFC days that a tradition began that continued for many years. Every Christmas Eve, Ford would sing "O Holy Night" and his bellowing voice would fill the sanctuary, declaring the appearance of the Christ child in the old carol. This was a tradition beloved by many in the congregation, not to mention the Reynolds family; one that would make celebrating Christmas Eve in the years to come seem incomplete without it.

Ping Pong

For decades, there was always a ping pong table at the farm, folded up in the corner of the room, ready to pull out to use as a large Thanksgiving table…or some serious games of ping pong.

There was no dispute in the family that Ford was the house champ, at least for a very long time. He would often play his children and though it would sharpen their skills, it was years before any of them could surpass dad. Heidi Jo remembers starting so young that she would have to jump up on the table to strike the ball, and would always have lines on her belly from the edge of the table when it was over.

His reputation as the man to beat wasn't just on Riverside Farm, mind you, as he would always remind the other leaders at CFC who the best was at elder retreats. It was often the same story when a younger leader would be added to the leadership team. "Oh, I can smoke this old man!" they would boast. And it would be the same result every time. The old guy wins.

Zeal for Evangelism

Ford had a passion for reaching souls, and employed it often during his years at CFC. He always sought to "make the most of every opportunity" and was never afraid to ask someone about the state of their soul.

One Sunday morning, as he was praying for people after the service, a woman almost seemed to run to the altar, and Ford asked her how he might pray for her. She said, "I don't know." Ford, not knowing what to pray, began to pray in tongues. The Spirit must have given the utterance, for wisdom and light dawned on the woman's heart in that moment. She realized that she needed salvation, and with Ford's help, confessed her need for Christ and placed her faith in Him.

After another service, an elderly Catholic woman came forward. Though she had a love for God, she confessed that she was missing something in her soul. She had learned a reverence for God in the Roman Church, and even obtained a moral compass, but did not think she knew Jesus personally in an authentic relationship. She had once thought that she would be saved through the sacraments of the mass, but now saw her need to place saving faith in the cross of Christ alone. Though Ford believed that some Catholics could certainly be "saved by grace" just as Protestants are, her uncertainty did not imbue the confidence of a true child of God. He was convinced, as had been his case, that there were many religious people who were not truly in Christ, and such, he believed, was the woman before him. He prayed with her to be saved, and her heart was radically converted. She never went back to the Roman Church again. In his experience in ministry, this was a rare, and delightful, conversion among those raised in the unregenerate forms of Catholicism.

Another Sunday, a man, being convicted, tears in his eyes, came to the altar for prayer. After some time of others praying for him, Ford asked the prayer workers if this man had ever received Christ. None that had prayed for him could say either way, so Ford asked him directly, "Do you want to receive Christ?"

"Yes!" came the answer.

The man didn't know how to express it, but he'd come to the front to be saved. Such experiences are why Ford was constantly bold, especially in his later years, never having a problem asking someone about the condition of their heart. "You've got to ask them the question!" he would say with a laugh.

Being the attendant at someone's eternal moment never became an old experience for Ford. He counted it a privilege and a blessing, and felt himself inserted with Christ's own disciples to whom the Master said, "Blessed are the eyes that have seen what your eyes have seen."

Full Gospel Businessmen's meetings were also places that he would lead people to Christ. Sharing his own testimony gave him the platform, credibility, and privilege of bowing his head with many to look to Christ for salvation.

Friendships with those in the Richville area also were used by the Lord for evangelism. An old friend, with whom Ford had once sung in the choir at United Church, came to saving faith during a visit Ford made to his home.

A local Sunday School superintendent, and at one time Ford's elementary school teacher, once sought out Ford to inquire as to what had changed in his life. The student became the teacher as he witnessed to her about Christ's saving work in his life and his story of being born again. Some of what he shared shook her and was outside of her experience. She went out and talked to her pastor about it and he affirmed her one-time student Ford's theology. She immediately sought a deeper conversion experience and confessed her faith in Christ alone. She desired to come out of mere mental assent to religious ideas and works righteousness, and find the witness of the Spirit in her soul. Later on, her public confession encouraged Ford, as he always felt that it was very important to confess with your mouth the Lord Jesus outwardly as evidence of your inward salvation.

On another occasion, Ford went to pray for a neighbor, a sick woman with a serious heart condition. She accepted the Lord and was so convinced of her healing that she began to testify to others about it.

There was also the story of a neighbor who, at one time, lived near Riverside Farm—one mentioned earlier in the book who had claimed to be a Christian, yet used to hide his cigarettes every time he'd see his clean-living, then-unsaved friend. Yet it was Ford who led the old man to Christ when he was well into his 90's. The late 1980's found him in a nursing home when Reynolds went to see him. "Friend," he said, "something has happened to me and the Lord changed my life. Can I pray for you?"

"It wouldn't do any good," the nonagenarian mumbled sourly. Ford postponed his prayer, and visited him again later on, this time walking him in his wheelchair. Once again, Ford witnessed to him about Christ's saving grace, and once again asked, "Can I pray for you? Would you like to put your faith in Christ?"

The old man said yes.

Ford prayed with him and the man's weak old voice repeated the words of this impromptu sinner's prayer. When finished, Ford said, "Praise God!"

His old friend agreed. "Yes! Praise God," he said. "Praise God indeed!"

Not long after this moment, Ford also led this man's sister to Christ. She was having heart trouble, and one day he stopped in to see her. Like her brother, she also placed her faith in Christ. After praying with her to receive salvation, Ford also prayed for her to be healed of her sickness. In the days that followed, she confessed to her family and friends that God healed her when that man Ford Reynolds prayed for her!

Running the day to day operations of Riverside Farm, he would find himself frequently interacting with businessmen from the community—other farmers, milkmen, equipment salesmen, insurance salesmen and the like; not to mention the hired men he had working for him at the farm every day. He did his best to share the gospel with anyone at any time he could. Once an insurance salesman prayed to receive Christ, and over the years several hired men came to faith along with some of their family members.

One humorous account was when Ford shared with a hired man's wife the testimony of a somewhat bizarre miracle that occurred in one of Langston's meetings before the evangelist came to northern New York. Another minister who had a gift of healing prayed for an obese woman who'd come to the altar. Langston explained to Ford that the heavy woman's skirt fell to the floor during the prayer as she seemed to supernaturally shed weight. Hearing the testimony, the hired man's wife beamed with excitement and declared, "I want to go to one of those meetings!" Eventually, she received Christ.

Sarah, the Missionary

Even Sarah found herself used greatly by God in evangelism. There was an elderly woman named Lenora who'd lost her husband. Her grieving was so heavy and so long that after four years, her doctor recommended that she see a psychiatrist. Meanwhile, she had a sister that was a vagabond, living out of a bag, supporting herself with monthly Social Security income, traveling on an unlimited bus pass from homeless shelter to homeless shelter. Lenora hadn't heard from her in years, and assumed her dead. Then one day, out of the blue, her prodigal sister called while she was working at Kinney Drugs and said, "I'm at the bus stop. Can someone pick me up?"

Sarah was shopping at Kinney's that same day and saw Lenora, who told her about her sister's sudden arrival. "What would you do with her?" Lenora asked her friend.

Sarah's answer came quickly. "I would take her to church."

CFC was hosting guest ministry that very week, and Sarah had hoped to bring someone along. She explained this to Lenora and asked if she would like to come.

Lenora said perhaps. They spoke of the possibility of Friday night.

Sarah went to the first two special meetings during the week (before the Friday service) and they were wild; so much so that it made Sarah uncomfortable and left her convinced that it wouldn't be wise to bring Lenora to such a gathering. The guest ministry at the church had a special focus on deliverance ministry, and there were many dramatic demonic manifestations happening in the meetings. Could God show a grieving, not-yet-Christian like Lenora the glorious truths of salvation by grace in such a charismatic environment?

Friday night would be the last meeting and Sarah did nothing to follow up with her friend. Lenora, however, didn't forget the invitation, and Sarah was shocked the doorbell rang right before she was about to leave for the service.

This night was as wild as the others. Contrary to what Sarah thought would happen, Lenora was deeply moved by the service. What affected her most was seeing the young people respond to the ministry. She'd been used to the absence and religious apathy of youth, and she was inspired by the spiritual fervor she saw in the young people at CFC. Further, she knew Ford and Sarah's children. Observing, albeit from a distance, the sincere and enduring faith of Laurie, Jamie, Jill, and Heidi Jo, she found herself convinced that, though all that she was experiencing at CFC was new and different, there must be something genuine in it.

Ford and Sarah began to persist in prayer for Lenora.

Not long after, during a Sunday service, she went forward after the message, as was the custom at CFC in those days, to receive prayer. Nothing much seemed to happen outwardly, but inwardly the Holy Spirit was working. Pastor Sinclair followed up with a personal visit a few days later, further explaining the gospel to her. She was encouraged by what she heard, but in God's mysterious and sovereign ways, it was still a few days later that her spiritual eyes were opened. She was alone, reading an entry from the common daily devotional *Our Daily Bread*, and suddenly, all was clear. She was a sinner; the cross of Jesus was her only hope; faith alone in Christ alone the way. It was a similar conversion experience to that of her friend Ford when, years before, gospel light broke into his heart while reading Kathryn Kuhlman books. All was new. Joy was real. She quickly drove down to Riverside Farm with her devotional in hand and, like a child who finds a treasure, said to Ford and Sarah, "Look at this!"

Faithful prayer had proven its power again. The Reynolds were reminded of Ephesians 1:16-18, and the need for the Holy Spirit to do what man cannot: "I do not cease to give thanks for you, remembering you in my prayers, that the God of our Lord Jesus Christ, the Father of glory, may give you the Spirit of wisdom and of revelation in the knowledge of him, having the eyes of your hearts enlightened..."

In her younger years, when still unmarried and working at the hospital, Sarah lived in Gouverneur. As her wedding date approached, she was gradually gathering resources to start her new homestead. One particular night, she went to a friend's home to get something her friend had promised to give her. When she arrived, the house seemed empty, so Sarah went against her nature (as she normally wouldn't enter an empty house), and made her way to the attic where she thought her item would be. Shocked she was to find her poor friend with a plastic bag over her head, delirious from sleeping pills, attempting to take her own life! Sarah's series of seemingly trivial decisions turned out to be the divine Hand of Providence. God had used her to save her friend's life. The woman recovered from her dark spell, and worked at the hospital for many years afterward, living well into her 90s.

Sarah's unsaved aunt also went to the Kathryn Kuhlman meetings in Pittsburgh. She was blind and though she didn't get saved or healed, the experience went like a seed into the ground. In God's sovereign ways, years later, she was very sick in a nursing home and called for her niece to come. The doctors pronounced her near death. Sarah went and sat by her side, reading Scripture to her. The hopeless doctors ordered a shot to ease the pain, but it never arrived.

And the woman didn't die.

Not long after, Ford and Sarah were in a Full Gospel Businessmen's meeting, and some acquaintances of the woman asked Sarah, "Were you the one that was in that room that night?" When Sarah said she was, they explained, "We all knew she was going to die. Her feet were blue! God performed a miracle."

Many years later, when this same aunt of Sarah's was in the care of a nursing home, Sarah went to see her for she was very sick again, and near death again. Sarah read the Bible to her, and prayed with her to trust in Christ. The new believer's countenance glowed. "He's wonderful, isn't he?" she said.

A seed sown years earlier had come into bloom.

Constantly sowing in others through evangelism and prayer, Ford and Sarah were always aware that they wouldn't see all the fruit of their ministry in their lifetime. That's why whenever God would let them see or hear a good report, like He did in this story, they would rejoice. They always saw it as an act of grace from a generous Father who knew his children needed encouragement.

Generous Giver

Ford was known as an extremely frugal man, a shrewd businessman, though also a generous giver. To his own estimation, the former allowed the latter.

Often people would come to him, knowing he had the means and the heart to help them. With prayer and trust in the Holy Spirit, he sought and employed great wisdom, often finding himself extending his hand as an answer to someone else's prayer.

He would lend, but would not strive with someone who wouldn't or couldn't pay him back. He practiced forgiveness rather than allowing money to create a relational barrier with friend or family. Eventually, he would not give unless he felt released in his heart to give it *freely* with no expectation of being repaid. Scriptures such as Christ's lessons on giving in the Sermon on the Mount became his guide: "But love your enemies, and do good, and lend, expecting nothing in return, and your reward will be great, and you will be sons of the Most High, for he is kind to the ungrateful and the evil" (Luke 6:35). Ford has no regrets about any gift he gave throughout the years, always giving "unto the Lord," not unto men.

With such faith, love, and generosity, he never found a lack of blessing or means in his own life. He was good with money, but always combined stewardship with a fierce faith that if he would tithe, give offerings when the Lord moved his heart, and give to those who had need, he would never lack. It wasn't until after he was converted that he began to give 10% of his income, as he believed this was the will of God for him.

The farm was very successful, and though there were other farmers who knew prosperity (like his own brother Dave), Ford Reynolds stood out in the community as a blessed man. He always had a good income, never wasted money on things or equipment he didn't need, and when he did buy something, he always did it with cash. Years later, when the author of this book asked him how much the monthly payments were on his car, he looked strangely at him, and said, "Payments?"

The man implemented two forms of wisdom. The first was the wisdom he had as a businessman. These were the principles, values, ethics, and philosophy that governed his heart and mind, affecting every decision he made every day about how to spend money. The second was the wisdom of the Holy Spirit instructing him what to do in every situation. This could be subjective, and required that he would be a man of prayer and have healthy communication with his wife. He would find himself often returning to this verse in James: "If any of you lacks wisdom, let him ask God, who gives generously to all without reproach, and it will be given him" (James 1:5).

He learned his frugal and shrewd business methods from his father, James. When asked about his business principles, Ford would always credit his father for demonstrating all of what he would one day practice himself. At the same time, he would always be careful not to simply point to men's good practices as the source of his blessing, but to the grace of God.

His father James left his children mineral rights that, over time, gave him some small income. On another occasion, he was included in a class action suit against an insurance company he had a policy with, and was compensated all that he'd paid in plus 6% interest. He received a check for $25,000. He immediately put this unexpected supply in a bank account with 17% interest. Within a few years, his investment began to grow.

Ford was also blessed by others who gave to him. Many saw him as a kind and honest man, worthy of favor, and it would often mean lesser fees or prices from those to whom he paid for goods or services.

Eventually, they'd be able to put all their children through college and have means to give them something once they married. Such was the fruit and responsibility of this generous man and his wife.

Early on in his walk with the Lord, he was watching a Rex Humbard crusade and sensed the Lord instructing him to give $2000. "Oh my goodness," thought Ford, "it must be the devil whispering in my ear!" After wrestling with this for quite a while, he finally concluded that the devil would not tell him to give $2000 to a gospel-preaching evangelist, and he sent the offering.

Such was the faith, the listening ear, and the obedience of this servant of the Lord. His willingness to give—and sometimes give *big*—to God's work was a consistent mark of his life.

Because of his obvious strength in stewardship and financial principles, along with the pattern of faith and generosity in his life, Ford was asked to serve as the chairman for CFC's 3-year capital campaign called "Growing in God" during the late 1980s. This would help CFC move to the next level of church expansion. Ford helped the church raise over $350,000, almost $50,000 of which he and his wife gave personally. The funds raised in this campaign would help them construct a new facility that would launch the church into a new season of growth.

A Family Man

He loved his children and was dearly loved by his children. Among the qualifications for eldership in 1 Timothy 3, it says that an elder "must manage his own household well, with all dignity keeping his children submissive, for if someone does not know how to manage his own household, how will he care for God's church?"

Ford and the leaders at CFC believed strongly in the idea that part of the ministry of an elder is that his family would become an example of a healthy Christian home. This was certainly the case for Ford and his family.

Though he was busy, he always had time for the family table, time for his children, and time for discipline.

A Peacemaker

Ford never hesitated in conflict. He knew and practiced the commands in Scripture to "make every effort to live at peace with all men" or "If your brother sins against you, go and tell him his fault."

He rarely spoke harshly—except perhaps to farm equipment—but had a gentle way in his attitude and speech. This was not weakness, mind you, but meekness marked by tender power. He was not afraid to confront, but "spoke the truth in love." His daughter, Heidi, has no memory of hearing her parents argue.

He was a peacemaker at heart, and would go out of his way to seek reconciliation. He was also willing to step in to help others resolve conflicts.

Mean-spirited, unreasonable people, or those unwilling to reconcile baffled him, as it was not his nature to divide or hold grudges. When wronged, he would embrace Christ's command to forgive with sobriety, and would be careful to hold that part of his heart up before the Lord until the sting subsided. He found blessing in living like this.

He had a friend named Thomas. He was a hard-working man, reasonable and generous; a man who tried to live by the golden rule. When he felt someone had not reciprocated the golden rule with him, however, he struggled to let go. He and Ford were very close until a certain incident brought a rift into their once-strong relationship.

With Ford's reference, a man from a nearby church named Scott borrowed Thomas' trailer and left a deposit as collateral. Part of the agreement was that Scott would also mow his property. When it went undone and the grass grew high, Thomas refused to give back the deposit. Finally, Scott borrowed a mower and cut the grass, but it was done so begrudgingly that lawn wasn't the only thing he cut—he also cut the electricity to the well pump, leaving Thomas and his family without water. Scott was so convicted that he confessed his sin to Ford, who encouraged him to apologize to Thomas. When Scott went to see the man, Ford agreed to accompany him, but Thomas would have nothing of forgiveness and reconciliation. In the end, he would not only hold this sin against Scott, but also against his old friend Ford.

Years later, as pastor of Richville Christian Fellowship, Ford preached one Sunday about the power of forgiveness and shared a story he'd read of a man healed of arthritis after he forgave someone that offended him. Unbeknownst to Ford, word reached Thomas of this sermon, and never before had Reynolds been so hated as he was by Thomas from that day forward, as his one-time friend assumed he was speaking of him.

By God's grace, however, the bitterness one day came to an end when Thomas' wife Cathy called and asked Ford to come over.

Reynolds went over to see his old friend and said, "Well, let me first say, if I've said anything or done anything, I want to ask you to forgive me." They began to talk and Thomas brought up the sermon, much to Ford's surprise. Ford explained that he had no intention that this message would be an arrow shot toward his old friend, but Thomas wouldn't hear it. His wife stepped in gently and said, "I forgive you, Ford..." then, turning to her angry husband, challenged him, "How about you?"

He considered this for a moment, and said, "I'll try."

Ford jumped right in and said, "That's good enough for me!"—adding his well-known jovial laughter. Thomas had leaned in an inch and Ford went the rest of the mile. From that day until the day of his death in 2003, Thomas was no longer angry with his old friend, and their relationship was restored to peace. For this, Reynolds was extremely grateful. He would frequently stop in for visits with Thomas, and the conversations were always full and friendly. It was like a miracle had happened. It was truly the power of forgiveness on display.

A Man of Prayer

The older Ford grew in the Lord, the more he learned the value of prayer. He would eventually become convinced that there would be no Christian success without prayer. It became part of his life, much like eating and drinking, until it naturally flowed from him almost involuntarily like a spiritual instinct. He understood Paul's encouragement to "pray in the Spirit at all times and on every occasion. Stay alert and be persistent in your prayers for all believers everywhere."

He also noted answers to prayer in the lives of others and used it as fuel for his own faith. Such a report came from a certain man named Herb Gardner that Ford knew during his days at United Church of Richville; a man with whom he'd actually sung in the choir years before. Neither man understood salvation by grace through faith at the time. Both eventually would!

Gardner had been delivering a load of flagstone for a sidewalk project he was working on in Trout Lake. The stone had to be delivered by boat. The load was so great, however, that the boat sank. As the vessel submerged below the surface, the life preservers drifted away and the poor man couldn't swim. His wife could swim, who was with him, but she was of no help to her dying companion, whose panicked flailing and strength were something she could not overcome. As he began the terrifying process of drowning, sinking below the surface several times, he used his brief moments on the surface to cry out desperate prayers. Suddenly, the life preserver drifted back to him, saving his life. He would later tell his friend Ford, "Don't tell me there isn't any God!"

After Ford's conversion, he went to visit his friend, whose heart was softened by such mercies, and explained the gospel to him. It was like ripened fruit, ready to be plucked from the branch. Gardner received Christ. Now he was rescued a second time—the first by life vest, the second by the cross!

Retelling the story often in the days that followed, Ford would laugh the laughter northern New York knows well, and he would use such a testimony to fuel his own faith.... *God hears prayer... God answers prayer... God's people ought to pray always and not give up.*

Regarding Prayer

Our humble hero learned much about prayer from his experiences, and from studying the Holy Scriptures. One point of learning was his practice of not praying lengthy prayers. He took Christ's words literally, who taught his disciples, "And when you pray, do not heap up empty phrases as the Gentiles do, for they think that they will be heard for their many words" (Matthew

6:7, ESV). To receive a miracle, he believed, a long prayer wasn't required. Therefore, he didn't see any point in belaboring his prayers, as if God would hear him if he just asked differently. If he did not see a miracle immediately, he would entrust the person's situation to the sovereignty and plan of God. Many times he would learn of miracles happening hours or days later. When, it would seem, nothing happened at all, he didn't mind asking again, like the story of Elijah and the rain in 1st Kings.

Another lesson learned in the gospels was the connection between prayer and the miraculous. He noted how Jesus walked on water (Matthew 14:22-33) just after he "went up on the mountain by himself to pray" (vs. 23). Surely, he reasoned, if this was the pattern and example our Master set for us, we ought not deter from it and expect success.

A Simple Man

Ford was a very intelligent man, yet always kept things simple. Mighty theological concepts would be boiled down to simple terms. Brilliant scholars who would teach with lofty vocabulary would not impress him. On the contrary, he would diagnose as arrogance that thing in a man that might delight in speaking above another's head. He saw it as the duty of the preacher to teach in a way that served the hearer in the hope of obtaining grace.

Further, Ford believed that hair-splitting disputes over secondary doctrine were foolish and outside of the debt of love Christians ought to have for one another. Similarly, he puzzled at charismatic chaos where disorder reigned and the Word was not given preeminence.

He had little grace for long services or long-winded preachers, especially when he was asked to share the message, only to have eager worship leaders, emcees, someone sharing a testimony abuse their liberty, leaving him with little or no time to deliver it.

Even a massive concept like discipleship was simple for him. It came down to simple obedience. Obedience in prayer. Obedience in tithing. Obedience in church attendance. Obedience in studying the Word. Yet, while holding these views, they were not contaminated by that legalism which spoils such spiritual activities.

His refreshing candor and bent toward simplicity might be demonstrated by his intervention in a situation where a local pastor had been falsely accused of impropriety by a divisive woman. She left his church and went to another, where she spread damning lies about him to her new pastor. Ford was invited to sit in a meeting where both pastors and the woman would try to sort this out and get to the truth. The new pastor, a man who knew Ford and his character, didn't know the accused man like Ford did.

With the common sense of a compass, Reynolds defended his friend and reasoned with the befuddled pastor, helping him see how the devil was using this woman. His words decimated the unlikely tales of the wicked woman and all came to light. Because of his simple wisdom and willingness to defend a friend, Satan had lost in his attempt to divide brothers and stain a good man's name. The wonderful principle from 1 John 1:7 defined this moment: *"But if we walk in the light, as he is in the light, we have fellowship one with another, and the blood of Jesus his Son cleanseth us from all sin" (KJV).*

It was like the Lord had used Ford to bring light into the situation, exposing darkness and sin, restoring fellowship and peace by "speaking the truth in love."

Spiritual Warfare

During his many years of ministry, Ford had seen a great deal of demonic activity affecting the lives of many poor souls. But he was never afraid, nor did he lack certainty that God could deliver anyone from the power of the devil.

His understanding of the believer's authority in Christ came during the days when he and Sarah hosted a weekly group in their home. He was greatly inspired by a book he read on deliverance ministry, and thought this approach ought to be a significant part of their ministry to others. During that time, he began to pray more often for the deliverance of those in bondage, taking authority in Christ's name over spirits that tormented and bound followers of Jesus.

He understood that a believer was indwelled by the Holy Spirit and could not be "possessed" by a devil, yet believed that a Christian could be *oppressed* by an evil spirit that sought to destroy faith, peace, and confidence. One woman confessed that she'd been involved in occult activity and had often joined in demonic levitation exercises. Tormented by a spirit, she asked Ford for prayer, who boldly rebuked the demon.

Another woman, significantly larger than Ford, screamed, "I hate you!" and charged at the gentle warrior. Unsure of her intentions, he pointed at her and shouted, "In Jesus' name!" and the woman fell flat on the carpet, disarmed by the power of God to lay a hand on him.

Though he would have powerful encounters like this, he would be frustrated if he wouldn't see enduring fruit from those who were delivered. As he studied the Scriptures, he saw Christ's words, "When the unclean spirit has gone out of a person, it passes through waterless places seeking rest, and finding none it says, 'I will return to my house from which I came.' And when it comes, it finds the house swept and put in order. Then it goes and brings seven other spirits more evil than itself, and they enter and dwell there. And the last state of that person is worse than the first" (Luke 11:24-26). He began to understand that deliverance ministry was not simply a power encounter, but a truth encounter. He understood the need for someone to repent and believe the gospel; to walk with God in a life of faith; to "submit yourselves therefore to God. Resist the devil, and he will flee from you."

One example of such ministry, and how Ford was trained by these experiences, was that of a lesbian that came to Langston and Ford for prayer. She believed she was tormented by a spirit[1]. When they began to pray, she screamed and shrieked in demonic agony that would rival most cinematic depictions. Afterward, she walked in victory for a time, but then went back to her lesbian

[1] This narrative is not to suggest that all same sex attraction is the result of demonization. Sometimes issues surrounding sexuality can have a traumatic history and be surrounded by much spiritual warfare, and this was such an encounter for Ford. In most cases, the author believes, being tempted by same sex attraction is as normal for some as heterosexual temptation is for others. The presence of it does not automatically indicate a demonic spirit or that the person should feel condemned with unique evil. "For all have sinned and fall short of the glory of God" (Romans 3:23).

relationship. Desiring to live a life of obedience to God, she returned to Langston and Ford, who prayed for her again. Just as it was the first time, she moaned, screamed, and shrieked in an awful manner. This time they were careful to instruct her in true repentance and faith. She turned away from sin, submitted her sexuality to Christ, and found freedom to live a new life. In the days and years that followed, her life changed dramatically. She eventually married a man and had children.

As Christian Fellowship Center continued to engage in "deliverance ministry" in the days that followed under the leadership of younger senior pastors, Ford was able to give insight into what the congregation was experiencing or observing, as he and Sarah had already walked through a season of encountering such spiritual warfare.

Spiritual Gifts

Besides the gift of healing, Ford also moved, though to a lesser extent, in other spiritual gifts, yet it would usually be in conjunction with his ministry of divine healing. For example, he would sometimes, though rarely, have a "word of knowledge." This phrase is taken from 1 Corinthians 12:8 and is sometimes referred to as a "sign gift," whereby someone will know something (usually about another person) that they would never have known otherwise, except by the Holy Spirit.

Back in the days of the chicken coop, Ford was leading worship (which he was known to do from time to time), and he had a word of knowledge that God wanted to heal some in the room with headaches. Another leader who was involved, more conservative about such things than Ford was, interrupted, thinking his brother to be getting carried away, and he redirected the service. Afterward, two men approached Ford, one a Canadian pastor, and said that their headaches ceased when the word of knowledge had been given. The word stirred their faith, and, reaching out for healing, they found their desire, and healing.

On another occasion, he felt impressed one Sunday morning to read 1 Thessalonians 4:14-16, something he rarely did: "We believe that Jesus died and rose again and so we believe that God will bring with Jesus those who have fallen asleep in him.

According to the Lord's own word, we tell you that we who are still alive, who are left till the coming of the Lord, will certainly not precede those who have fallen asleep. For the Lord himself will come down from heaven, with a loud command, with the voice of the archangel and with the trumpet call of God, and the dead in Christ will rise first. After that, we who are still alive and are left will be caught up together with them in the clouds to meet the Lord in the air. And so we will be with the Lord forever. Therefore encourage each other with these words."

Some remarked after the service that Ford's word seemed strange in the context of everything else that had been done and said in that service.

That night, a young man in the church named John Flack and his fiancé Mary were in a terrible car accident, and the young woman went home to be with the Lord. She had been Ford and Sarah's oldest daughter Laurie's best friend. The word Ford had given from Scripture that morning became a great comfort to the church and to his own family, helping them to recognize the sovereign will of God in this matter. In His mysterious ways, he had allowed this for His own glory, and was kind enough to tell the saints at CFC about it so they might be comforted.

Flack was hospitalized with severe injuries, and Grampa Wells went in and prayed for him. He told him, "You're going to be out of here a lot faster than the doctors are saying." And he was.

And the Lord also used Grampa Wells at the Laramay funeral, when he asked a young man named Michael, "If you were to die today, do you know if you would go to heaven?" Michael wasn't sure, and he'd seen something in the believers at Laramay's wake and services that he hadn't seen before–an unusual peace in the midst of tragedy. He couldn't explain it. That night he received Christ.

Family Miracles

In 1991, Ford's daughter Jill and her friend were hit almost head on by a drunk driver. She cracked her pelvis in three places, and her parents were told that she would need plastic surgery to repair her damaged ear. Father and mother prayed, specifically remembering the miracle of Malchus in Gethsemane, when Jesus healed him after Peter cut off his ear in a rage. When hospital staff took Jill to the operating room the next morning, they were shocked to see that "things were not as bad as they had originally thought." The doctor stitched her up and that was it. The ear would eventually heal so well that one could not tell it had ever been so severely damaged.

Jill laid in a bed for almost a month before she could even sit up, her legs nearly atrophied, and questions remained about her future, specifically her ability to walk again and have children. The Lord was with Ford and Sarah (and their suffering daughter), giving them daily strength and faith to pray. The pain was vicarious for both of them, as their hearts ached to see their girl in so much agony. In the end, God healed her completely, and she would one day give them three grandchildren and become a runner.

All of this would sometimes lead Ford to ask the question: *What do you give credit to God for? Would Jill have improved without prayer? Was every positive outcome to be credited to the God of heaven?* What about reports among the heathen, who do not pray or have faith, who see the tide swing for and against them when diverse illnesses or afflictions come upon them? Is God to be credited for those who improve, even among these? Ford would say yes. He believed the broad sweeping truth found in James 1:17 which declares, "Every good gift and every perfect gift is from above, coming down from the Father of lights with whom there is no variation or shadow due to change." He also believed in common grace, that all mankind are the beneficiaries of God's kindnesses, though they love him not, "For he makes his sun rise on the evil and on the good, and sends rain on the just and on the unjust" (Matthew 5:45).

Life on the Farm

Days on Riverside Farm in these years were days of hard work, simple living, and making good family memories. Ford would often think about how wise his grandfather was to buy the 265 acres, level, tillable, and free from rocks. It also included a beautiful sandbar on the Oswegatchie River where everyone learned to swim and enjoyed so much family time together. The

Reynolds cherished the farm life and were grateful for what a wonderful place it was to raise children.

Haying Time

Haying time was always accompanied with a hot July sun, lots of sweat, and tired muscles. Ford would put his nose to the grind and try to get all the fields cut and baled as quickly as possible. The sooner the hay made it to the barn, the better the quality. He would barely even take a lunch break during these days. It was mowing in the morning and baling in the afternoon. A good part of the afternoon work was collecting the bales for storage in the barn.

August was the second cutting.

The kids provided much of the manpower needed to make the venture a success. They would mix work with joking and jesting, water breaks, and popsicles. They would also play pranks on the hired men, like the time they put a snake on the tractor seat of the unsuspecting farmhand, and nearly had to resuscitate him when he saw it! The Reynolds children had little knowledge at the time of what fond memories they were making. They would relive these moments often in the years to come.

Eldon Wilson, a frequent guest at Christian Fellowship Center, rightly said of farmers during haying season, "When the time is ripe for haying, don't expect anything from a farmer except what he's doing on the farm!" Pastor Sinclair concurred, and would give great grace to his farmer-elder-friend when the demands of summer on the farm came calling.

One would know it was haying time by just looking at the tough-skinned farmer, his arms a deep brown from tanning, and a "farmer's tan" on his neck line that resembled the sun hitting half the moon.

In the author's early days of courting the family, he was put into the hay mow with his interest, Heidi Jo, to work the bales. Ford and Sarah joked that this was his first day of fulfilling seven years of labor to earn his bride. At the end of the day, in the 110 degree barn, sweating, itching, and coughing from inhaling chaff, hoping the last load had come in, the young suitor asked Heidi Jo, "Is Laban still out there in the field?"

Ford had a strong conscience about honoring the Lord's Day, and even when demands seemed beyond his capacity, he wouldn't work on Sunday except for the work that *had* to be done on the farm, like milking the cows. The 260-acre property would sit quietly on that day while tractor engines roared in adjacent fields. But he believed he could accomplish more in six days of hard work and resting on the seventh than by striving in his own strength for seven days. God always honored this simple expression of trust and dependence upon Him as Ford never seemed to lack a thing, and the work always got done.

The family was always rewarded after haying season with a family vacation. Sites in Vermont, Maine, and New Hampshire were common destinations, which often included hotels, pools, and pretty mountains. The kids loved the adventure as they'd put the cap on the back of the pickup truck, throw a mattress in, and have their own private clubhouse for the entire duration of the road trip (such a paradise would never be allowed today, of course).

The Reynolds children have many fond memories of family vacations and the time they would have with parents and siblings. One that stands out was the trip that began on the wrong foot—literally. The night before departing for Disney, their father dropped a crowbar on his foot, nearly crushing it. This malady forced him to walk around the theme park in a big boot, and how glad we was that he didn't have to work on the farm in such a condition. Though a sad sight at the time, the enduring memory of their limping patriarch would later in life bring laughter even to their adult children as the Reynolds siblings would reminisce (around many a family table) about their time with dad at Disney that summer.

Though farms are known to be dangerous places, the Lord kept the Reynolds family from tragedy and any great harm, and for that they were very thankful. There were incidents, however, near misses, and miracles that would remind them of the strong and kind hand of God working in their days.

Once a wagon was loaded with hay, especially if the sky looked foreboding, everyone knew that the goal was to get the dry hay into the barn as quickly as possible. Jamie was known to fly through the fields, the wagon bouncing over humps and ruts, kicking up dust that would fill his wake, until he reached the barn. Once, when younger, he wasn't driving, but riding on the very top of a full load of hay while a hired man blazed through the field like he would one day do. However, the wagon tipped over—a frightening experience—but young Jamie walked away unscathed. That evening, his heart still rejoicing in the providence of protection he'd been afforded, he stubbed and smashed his toe in the house. This reminded him that one can stumble in the yard and perish, or fall from a bridge and live…if grace were not at the helm.

The Reynolds were not "dualists"—separating sacred from secular in such a way that blinded them to God's interest in their farm or how useful it was for spiritual things—but, like the Celts in the days of St. Patrick, the Reynolds learned to bring God into their daily work, committing it unto Him and turning to Him when needs arose.

Once, during haying season, a baler broke, and Ford expressed his frustration to Sarah, explaining that he could fix it, but it would take a few hours he didn't have. Sarah prayed, and was delighted a few minutes later to hear the hum of the baler as work continued.

The baler broke again on the 4th of July one summer, an untimely breakdown, as local repair shops and supply stores were closed. So Ford waited for a local farmer, Frank LaFalts, to finish his work, and finally borrowed his baler at 3 p.m. He worked until 7 p.m. and got it all done. They later found out that there was a downpour from 3-7 p.m. all around them, but the Lord had restrained the adverse weather, which would have ruined the hay.

Another year, Ford had cut down two fields of hay on a Thursday, planning to load it into the mow over the following two days, but Friday brought rain. That meant that two fields of hay would all have to be brought in on Saturday, an enormous task. Sarah found herself in the barn, straining through the heat and back-breaking work, determined with the rest of her family to get the job done. As the day plodded along, she grew weak and light-headed. The task seemed to be too much, and she longed for help. Suddenly, she saw her younger brother Richard in the driveway. His appearance shocked and frightened her, seeing that, in this youthful season of his life, responsibility and service were not his chief virtues. Sarah assumed trouble with mother. "Is Mom alright?" she asked, visibly concerned.

"Calm down, calm down," Richard assured, "everything's fine. I just saw Ford out there in that wet field and I thought maybe you'd like some help!"

This seemed a miracle to Sarah, not only because God sent help just in time, but also because, in this season of her younger brother's life, he was the last person she might expect to spontaneously come offer his services! God had clearly, in Sarah's estimation, moved on his heart.

Richard worked in the mow all afternoon and even into the night until all the hay was brought in from the fields. In all, it was 1500 bales of hay in one day!

So, to the Reynolds, they saw that God could fix the machinery, hold back the weather, protect their family, and even send help when it was needed. They even found the goodness of God to be their guide in helping them find lost cows and calves.

Little miracles were often seen, and needed, during times when cows would give birth. The soon-to-be mothers would sometimes go into hiding when delivering, leaving their masters to find them. On a 250-acre farm, this could be like finding a needle in a haystack, especially since the heifers didn't want to be found. The "hunting" duty would often fall to Sarah, as Ford had to tend to the milking. She learned to pray during these times, knowing that her best compass was the Holy Spirit, who knew exactly where the animals were. More than once, moved by what she felt to be the leading of the Spirit, she would go down a path in a certain direction, and Ford, on days he was able to assist, would sometimes say, "You don't need to go down there. I've already checked."

And there would be the animal!

On one occasion, Sarah found herself deep in the woods, fighting through briars and prickers, wondering why she'd ended up in such a place. She'd asked the Lord to lead her, but surely the cow she was searching for could not be in such a place. Then she heard the moaning of the animal in travail, lying in the thick on sharp thorny bushes. God had indeed led her again!

Such stories would provide plenty of laughter and thankfulness in the years that followed. Remembering these days,

Sarah would say with a grin, "As I'd go out looking in the fields, sometimes I'd ask myself, 'Now where was it that Ford told me not to go?' And I'd go there!"

The idea of praying for even the simplest things on the farm became a way of life for the children. As an adult, Heidi Jo would cite her farm days as that which taught her that God is interested in even the most menial things, and that prayer should be as natural as breathing.

Ford had to get used to the rhythm and flow of farm life interacting with church life. Sometimes the interruptions were not controllable. He would learn to roll with the challenges, and most of the time laugh his way through. One night, his prayer group gathered at his house at 7 p.m. and a cow was in labor over the hill beyond the house. He assisted the birth of the calf, and then went inside and washed up for the prayer meeting, which finally started at 9 p.m.!

Bulls

One source of several miraculous stories in Ford's life on the farm was the ever-precarious and dangerous relationship he had with bulls. These animals were necessary to procreate more calves and rounded out the social life of the farm, but due to their size and temperament they often posed a threat. Ford always removed the horns of his bulls, so he could avoid such tragedies as befell his farmer-friend down the road, who was gored to death in a pen.

When a bull would get aggressive and cranky, Ford referred to them as "ugly," and had to face down such an unpredictable creature more than once. He would always do so with a stick in hand. Every beast knew his voice, and when he had a stick in hand, he was in charge. On one occasion, being in a hurry on a Sunday morning, Ford neglected to grab a stick as he normally would.

The bull got ugly.

The cows had been out in the open meadow, where they could feed on the plush green grass for a while, a common location for the herd, where Ford would corral them back into the pasture which would contain them in tighter, safer quarters farther from the road.

On this day, the hired man accompanied his boss into the meadow to help move the animals, but the bull did not want to go into the pasture.

Ford hollered at his beast, but the creature stood its ground in the meadow. The monster wasn't afraid of his master's voice this time; not without a stick in hand.

Then it charged.

Ford put his hand on its nose, a last-ditch effort to command some authority, but it was too late. The rest was a blur.

The hired man looked on, frozen with fear as Ford's body went flying through the air like a rag doll. He landed with a crushing thud on the unforgiving ground, and the attack continued as the enraged beast slammed its nose into its victim's side, rolling him like a barrel, over and over, across the field.

The hired man felt helpless to intervene.

Suddenly, for no logical reason, the bull stopped. This was completely against the bull's instinct and nature. It had Ford right where it wanted him—with 1600 pounds of muscle, it could step on its 150-pound victim and crush his chest easily, but the creature seemed to be looking into the air at something formidable that stood in the way of his attack. Ford would always be convinced that there was an angelic intervention.

He stood to his feet, wondering if he would be able to do so from an unknown injury he may have sustained, but one would never have known that the ugly bull had ever touched him. Not only did he not have a scratch or a sore spot on his body, he didn't even have a grass stain on his clothes!

It was a miracle.

Ford and the hired man had quickly left the field, got the farm truck, and went back to corral the bull into the pasture with a little more horsepower. Then the farmer went back to the house, got ready for church, and went to CFC to teach Sunday School.

It wasn't until after church that he told Sarah about the attack.

This story he would tell and retell in the years to come, often remembering the goodness of God, and how differently life might have been for the Reynolds family had God not intervened. He would often say, "Thank God for my guardian angel."

The day after his salvation from the wrath of the bull, the animal was on the truck to the butcher. And the story was always a reminder of the gospel, how another Guardian Angel came to rescue all who would receive Him from the wrath of God. The farm and farm life was full of gospel pictures, not unlike the One who used many farming pictures in His parables many years ago.

Other family members have their own stories of being terrorized by these monsters made of beef. On one occasion, Sarah was out in the field with the youngest, 14-year-old Heidi Jo, searching the fringe of the woods for a heifer that had just given birth, as the animals would often hide themselves there. Ford went deeper into the forest to look, and once he was separated from the women, the bull noticed that they were alone. Without the alpha there, the creature's instincts must have told him that the ladies were vulnerable, so he made straight for them. Terrified, they went deeper into the woods themselves, as it would be unlikely (and unusual) for a bull to follow them there.

But it did.

Hiding behind a thicket of bushes and trees, Sarah told her daughter to take a peek to see if they were in the clear. When Heidi Jo craned her head around the corner of a bush, she found herself face to face with the angry creature. "He's right there!" she yelled. "Run!"

"Let's climb a tree!" commanded her mother.

Like a cat with a dog on its heels, they scaled the tree faster than green grass through a goose. Heidi Jo crouched on a lower limb, just a foot or so above the enraged beast that now stood below them staring up at what it hoped would become its victims.

Ford heard the cries of his women and came running, stick of power in hand, shouting in the tone he used only with the bull, "Geeeet aggghhhtta here!!!"

The animal obeyed and the girls were saved. But that was a close call.

Hired Men

As the children grew older and would gather at holidays around the family table, some of the memories that would draw the greatest laughter was the recollection of the many stories of hired men on the farm.

"Hired men" were often hard workers and good with their hands, though it was uncommon to find a man whose strength was his intellectual prowess. For example, one hired man was caught stealing gas from the pump in the driveway, but claimed he'd swerved to the pump to avoid a cat. That didn't explain how fifteen gallons were missing from the gas reservoir! The same man had a wrench set stolen from him, but confessed with a smile to Ford, "That's no problem, because I got the 5-finger discount on that anyway." (He'd stolen it in the first place.) Another hired man arrived at work and reported to Ford that he'd seen his rabbit breed with his duck, and then declared, "We're gonna have some strange looking animals back up'ere!"

So many funny memories.

A certain worker, the family discovered, could burn through a cigarette like paper in a furnace. One day, Sarah saw the milk going down the drain in the milk house (as someone had forgotten to close the spigot), so she quickly reported it to the hired men in the field. They sprinted to the milk house like it was an Olympic track meet, and by the time they arrived, the smoker already had a lit cigarette in his mouth! Though an unhealthy habit, it was mildly impressive to think of what skill it might take to locate and light a cigarette while in a dead sprint!

Work on the farm would have been impossible without these men, who sometimes ran the whole farm in Ford's absence. Mike Blackmur was the best hired man Ford ever had, a hardworking man who was kind to the children. He served the family farm for years along with others.

Some hired men, or at least circumstances that accompanied them, were downright strange, like the time a new worker borrowed the farm truck to move into the "hired man house" a mile up the road. He took the truck as planned and moved in, but never reported to work the next morning. When Ford went up to check on him after the no-show, he found the truck in the driveway and the house vacant. He'd moved out on the same night he moved in!

And there were others.

Pete and Sue arrived in their family vehicle, a hearse. They moved into the hired man house, but as it turned out, they were not married. That would not do for a godly man like Ford, who would not tolerate blatant fornication in a home he owned. He gently explained to Pete that an employee could not have a cohabiting partner living in his house. The man understood, and married his girlfriend right away, if not just to keep his job. Ford's ultimatum must have angered the woman though, as she called Sarah and made up a story that neighbors claimed to have seen their husbands out in town with other women. Such a thought could not have been more preposterous to Sarah. Her husband had his sins, but partying with the ladies into the night wasn't one of them!

The woman, however, was persistent with her tales. She called again on another night, trying to disguise her voice, posing as a mistress, expressing her romantic affections for Ford, trying to upset Sarah. But Sarah immediately knew who it was.

Sue would also accompany Pete to assist him at the farm, quite poorly one should know, unable to lift a single bale. The Reynolds were uncertain as to her motive, though it seemed she were either performing for a job *or* trying to seduce Ford as her clothing was often minimal. Her audition ended one night when she tried to help with the milking, clad in skimpy, cut off shorts. While they worked, she'd left her two-year-old son in their hearse, who put the vehicle out of gear, causing the long black car to roll across the driveway into the meadow. Minutes before, the young Reynolds children were in the very path of the hearse! Sarah was beside herself with frustration and anger. It was decided. Sue would not be welcome on the farm anymore. It wasn't long afterward that she left Pete, who very quickly had another woman move in with him. Soon Pete was gone too, as he knew he couldn't have a live-in girlfriend, and the Pete & Sue era had come to an end.

Of course the hired men knew that Ford was a man of faith, and would often tailor their conduct and speech to accommodate him when they were around him. Telling a story about his weekend, one hired man corrected himself mid-sentence in a conversation with Ford, knowing he wouldn't allow alcohol-fueled parties at the hired man house, saying, "Yessir! They were going to have a parrr...barbecue..."

For years afterward, the term "par-barbecue" was permanently added to the Reynolds vocabulary.

Another hired hand requested to bring his dog over to the farm to accompany him while he worked. "Is it male or female?" Ford asked. The man looked puzzled for a moment as he tried to remember, and then in a moment of inspiration explained to Ford, "Well, I know its mother was female!"

Not to be outdone, another man that had worked the farm for a few years was bragging about how many important people had attended his birth. The volume and pitch of his voice were reaching a crescendo as he passionately explained the royal roll of dignitaries that honored him by attending his arrival to the world. Politicians and celebrities, family and friends were all present; much like those who attended the manger, so many would not miss the birth of such a great man. Ford played along. "Was the general there?" he asked.

"Yes!" he explained.

"And the governor?"

"Oh yes! He was there!" he insisted.

"What about your mother?"

The man was lost in his fantasy, and answered without a blink, "Oh yes! She was there, too!"

Another man, who incidentally didn't end up working out as a permanent fixture on the farm, couldn't remember anything he was ever told to do. One day, he had to make an important call home, but couldn't remember his own phone number. These were days without cell phones, and most people knew their phone numbers as well as they knew their own names. Ford knew the man's number and gave him the information, but by the time he walked the fifty steps to the barn phone, he'd forgotten. Finally, Ford wrote it down for him, and he successfully made the call.

Ford loved these men and treated them with fatherly grace, often minding matters of their lives off the farm, being sure they were taken care of. He was not a hard man to work for, but was a benevolent employer—fair and good and kind, yet not allowing excuses for lazy or poor labor. He knew the value of hard work, and expected no less from his employees.

One of the brighter farmhands was a young man from Chile named Sergio that needed work just to immigrate to the U.S. He was at one time a political prisoner because he had spoken out against the Chilean government, and he was now seeking sanctuary in the U.S. It so happened that he needed work simultaneously with Riverside Farm needing a worker. Ford hired him, and although he caught on to things quickly, he would sometimes not pay attention to details. Sarah recalls the horror of the moment he whipped around the corner of the barn on a tractor, racing down the hill from the haymow, pulling a trailer at an ungodly speed. He'd put his foot on the clutch instead of the brake, smashing the farm speed record around the milkhouse!

He was a kind man, especially to the children, carving a Viking ship for Jamie and a squirrel for Sarah with astonishing craftsmanship. He'd mastered such a craft while a prisoner in Chile.

And the stories seem endless, the ballad of hired men who bungled, stammered, and stumbled their way into the minds and hearts of the Reynolds clan. Men who mowed over little Heidi Jo's cat Noose and broke her heart; hit another cat with a car and put the wet, injured feline down into the feed hole to claim that a terrible fall had afflicted it; backed over another cat with a tractor and put it under the large icicles behind the milk house, claiming it had been crushed; ran over an expensive thermos and threw it in a ditch instead of fessing up; men who demanded more to work for less. Others adorned the tenant house with psychedelic paints or lived in unthinkable filth, clutter, or disarray. Cleaning up the house between hired men was always an arduous task and useful, the children who helped clean might be led to believe, for their sanctification. Cigarette smoking, animals in the house, and neglect would often lead to daunting duties, bad memories, and sometimes the renovation of the entire interior of the house.

Ford always did his best to bring these men and their families to Christ, and many of them found their faith ignited or growing while under Ford's authority. Even so, Ford was relieved when he didn't have to hire farm hands anymore.

Full Gospel Businessmen's Fellowship

We've already mentioned that Full Gospel Businessmen's Fellowship had a significant place in Ford's life and story. He first heard about Full Gospel through a friend that had attended one of their events in New York City. Kathryn Kuhlman had been a guest at their conference, and this piqued his interest. Founded by author of a well-known book *The Happiest People On Earth*, businessman Demos Shakarian, the vision of Full Gospel was:

> *To reach men in all nations for Jesus Christ,*
> *To call men back to God,*
> *To help believers to be baptized in the Holy Spirit and to grow spiritually,*
> *To train and equip men to fulfill the Great Commission,*
> *To provide an opportunity for Christian fellowship,*
> *To bring greater unity among all people in the Body of Christ.*

When Ford found out that this international organization had a chapter in Watertown only 45 minutes south, he went to visit.

He immediately felt a connection and joined the chapter. This ministry would play a significant role in Ford's life for years, giving him a wider platform for his ministry work of evangelism and divine healing.

In one meeting, as was the custom at Full Gospel meetings, they prayed for anyone who wanted to receive ministry at the end of the gathering. The president of this particular chapter was praying over a large man of 6'5" stature, and Ford stood at his behind him to join in prayer. Suddenly, Ford's hands got tense and warm, and he was convinced the Holy Spirit was empowering him to pray. As he laid his hands on the tall man, the giant fell to the ground like a dead man.

And he was there for a long time.

Ford had brought a guest with him, a southern Baptist pastor, who had never witnessed an event such as this, and he stared in amazement at the large man on the ground. The fallen man lay there so long, Ford and his friend actually left the meeting while he was still prostrate.

At the next Full Gospel meeting a month later, Ford inquired as to what had happened to this man. The chapter president explained that the man had previously had an illness in his eyes, but when he arose from the floor that day, he was healed! Ford wasn't surprised, as he'd sensed the healing power of the Holy Spirit "on his hands" that day when he had prayed for him.

Nothing like that happened to the farmer-evangelist before or since.

He saw this experience as another of several inaugural signs; an affirmation of the call upon him to pray for the sick. In the days that followed, he shared his testimony and prayed for the sick in Full Gospel chapters in Lowville, Gouverneur, Indian Lake, Malone, Lake Placid, Saranac Lake, Ogdensburg, Lowville, Carthage, Pulaski, and even Ottawa, Canada.

Ford had preached in Indian Lake, New York, and things went as they normally would—worship and personal testimony followed by prayer. Afterward, a woman approached him and said joyfully, "I was healed tonight! I really was!" He later discovered that the woman, wife of the chapter president, had been ill for a long time. Though she only said her problem was "personal," Ford suspected that it was female-related. Without even receiving prayer, she asked the Lord to heal her, and then visited the bathroom to discover that she was cured! This was cause for great rejoicing in her family and in the Full Gospel chapter. Ford was so blessed that he refused to accept the honorarium he was offered. He'd already received his reward and his heart was full!

Eventually, he was instrumental in starting a chapter in the Gouverneur area and became the chapter president. He enjoyed the way this organization brought together believers from different churches and denominations, as well as its impact on the unsaved. Their monthly meetings would often include the elements of worship, a speaker who would share a personal testimony, and then conclude with a time of prayer for salvation and the filling of the Holy Spirit. Stories of conversions and miracles would abound during this time, many of them as the direct result of Ford's ministry. Being in that environment gave him great faith as he preached and prayed, if not only because those who would attend the meetings came with great expectation.

When Ford spoke in a Watertown meeting, he brought Sarah along. After she introduced herself as "Sarah Reynolds" to those sitting at her table, a nearby woman said, "Well, that's the speaker's name. Are you related to him?"

Sarah nodded.

"Oh!" the woman remarked to the others around the table, beaming. "We're sitting with the speaker's wife!"

Sarah would both laugh and rejoice at this, remembering the days when he was unconverted.

His most memorable meeting was in Lowville, New York. The Holy Spirit gave him "unction" as he shared his personal testimony, and then there was an enormous response for altar prayer. Some could not seem to get off the floor, and others were healed of sicknesses. When the meeting ended, the chapter president said, "We fasted and prayed, and look what God did!"

Reynolds never forgot that evening, nor the lessons learned about the value of fasting and prayer.

In all, he was involved with Full Gospel for close to 15 years.

So, the farmer-evangelist enjoyed many fruitful years of ministry through Christian Fellowship Center and Full Gospel. But as the seasons change on the farm, so do the seasons change in one's life. This farmer would soon become a church planter and lead pastor.

Others' Recollections and Thoughts

The man was a bulwark for those around him during the CFC years, perhaps incarnating the prophetic principle that if one is faithful with little, he'd be trusted with much. He proved himself reliable and helpful in the work of the ministry during these years. Young Pastor Sinclair was greatly appreciative of the stability and friendship that his older friend brought to the table.

"There's always been a rock solid sense of faith in Ford—just believing God," Sinclair would say of this season. "It was evidenced in many ways—certainly his eagerness to pray for people to see God meet them, but in a broader sense it was evidenced in his confidence that God was going to move. It didn't matter what happened, when everybody in the room was shaken by circumstances, tragedies, or financial setbacks, or conflicts, Ford was always rock solid in his faith. You could always count on him to laugh and say, 'God's got this under control.'"

In the numerous circumstances that would hit the shores of the church, Sinclair found strength in his elder-brother. "The sense that 'this boat is gonna float' just oozes out of him," remembers Sinclair. "His attitude was always, 'Heaven and earth will pass away, but His words won't.' And that sense of stability just oozes out of him in all kinds of circumstances. That then spills into what it imparts in everyone around him—especially to me as a young pastor: confidence. We could be confident in the midst of circumstances that could otherwise shake me, shake our leaders, or the congregation. He really brought something that was very powerful."

The fruit of it all was friendship, an oft rare gift to a pastor, and Sinclair was blessed by it. "Doing all that in a way that made you know that he was in your corner, that he was supportive, that he was behind you, was really quite profound."

As any pastor worth his salt, Sinclair had his own challenges and battles early on in the pastorate, but his old friend was right by his side. "I remember my first meeting with the leadership team," he recalls. "Ford basically vocalized that he believed God's hand was on me. And he did it in a way that gave me confidence, because I knew at that time that not everybody believed that. That was very significant to me."

Ford had the ability to acknowledge someone's weaknesses while at the same time recognizing God's grace at work in the imperfect vessel. It was a gift of discernment and perception that built up the Body, kept him from stumbling over flaws, and gave those who led him the security of knowing he was with them regardless of their particular flaws.

Sinclair once brought in an evangelist from Canada that had a charismatic flair that was off-putting to some. However, while the Holy Spirit moved during the meeting, Reynolds looked across the altar at his young friend Rick and said, "God is using this boy!"

Sinclair also marveled at the kindness and compassion Ford would show his wife when dark clouds would sometimes fall on her soul. This tenderness would have an enduring impact on him, setting an example for him of a man who loved his wife "as Christ loved the church" (Ephesians 5:25).

Sinclair also grew to appreciate Reynolds' Pentecostal passions. "Ford Reynolds was like a bloodhound on the scent of power gifts," he noted. It seemed no meeting would be complete for Reynolds until they prayed for the sick. He would often provoke the congregation to that, and in doing so, helped shape the culture of the church into one that not only gave God an opportunity to perform signs and wonders, but also one that had great faith that He would, and could, do it. Even when Sinclair "doubted that the wind was blowing," Ford would prod him to welcome people for prayer at the altar, and there would, many times, be obvious answers to prayer and testimonies of divine healing.

"He was like a one-man healing ministry," remembers Pastor Sinclair. "And he wouldn't take no for an answer!"

Until he started the church in Richville, Ford's gifts were often not on display on the platform during Sunday morning services, but his presence still loomed large, his influence making a major contribution to building a movement at CFC and among church plants in their circle. "Probably most people don't realize what he provided," Sinclair added. "The penchant, even today, toward the gifts of the Spirit and the move of God is a tribute to his persistence and zeal in that area. The burning bush never went out."

In an American culture that seems to drift toward the intellectual and the academic, Ford Reynolds was there—a man that grew up in intellectual, but dead, religious experience—always encouraging the Body at CFC to keep their hearts open to the move of God by the Holy Spirit.

"There are some movements and churches that have a great fireplace but no fire," reflects Sinclair. "There are other movements and churches that have a great fire but no fireplace. A fireplace with no fire is cold. There's no life-giving warmth in it. A fire with no fireplace is dangerous. That's a formula for houses burning down. In some ways, a fireplace with a fire—Ford Reynolds is the type of man that keeps you on track with the pursuit of the fire. If CFC is a 1st Corinthians 12 church today, and if there was one person that I would say was instrumental in keeping us on track with that 1st-Corinthians-12-gifts-of-the-Spirit aspect, that one person would be Ford Reynolds. People might not know that. As many people have honored him in northern New York, he's largely an unsung hero. CFC has maintained a sense of life in large part because of him, but also our impact as a Body on the region is felt. So in some ways, he really has been a key player in shaping God's move in our area although his name might not be the one that's mentioned."

Mike Tomford, an assistant pastor at CFC for years, and currently pastor of the church Reynolds planted, Richville Christian Fellowship, also has fond memories of Reynolds. "I've known Ford Reynolds my entire Christian life," he said. "He was an elder in Madrid when I came on the scene as a SUNY Potsdam college student at 21 years of age. I remember him being so steady and consistent. He would have been in his 50's when I met him. As a young Christian on an emotional roller coaster at times, he was an example to me of a steady man."

Ford had always been known for his laughter, and it was no different at CFC. "One thing I appreciate about the man is his joy. It was very genuine and pretty contagious. His laugh is pretty well-known around upstate New York."

As Pastor Tomford attended Sunday school classes at CFC, he would observe Reynolds' simple approach to Scripture and the faith he had that God would do what He promised. He also remembers the stunning example of generosity set by his elder during the "Growing in God" campaign in the late 1980s, as many were encouraged to publicly proclaim their faith pledges in the hope of inspiring others. Tomford, a part-time handyman at the time and not used to having much money in his hands, watched as some stood up and voiced their decision to give. One man said he'd give $5/week toward the building campaign, another said she'd give a certain amount, and then another. The congregation praised God not only for the provision, but for the obedience of God's people to give by faith. Without fanfare or boasting, Ford reluctantly shared the testimony of the private battle he had in his heart with the Lord, knowing the first number he chose was too small, and the number kept increasing, higher and higher, until he settled on giving $50,000 to the church. "For a college student making $4/hour," reflects Tomford, "I was blown away not only at the number but at the generosity."

Reynolds was known, by some, as being frugal and tighter than the bark on a tree. "He remembers prices of small, sometimes obscure things from years back," notes his daughter Heidi Jo. "He even remembers the price of gas on their honeymoon!"

But even with his frugality, he had a reputation in and out of the church for being generous. "I always appreciated his generosity," says Tomford, who was able to observe it in many ways and contexts throughout the years. "That's always inspired me about Ford."

Even during the writing of this book, the 91-year-old Ford Reynolds asked Tomford how people were doing financially during the coronavirus pandemic. Tomford, now a lead pastor, explained the landscape of the Body in this regard. Ford handed him some money and said, "Please give this to whoever needs it, at your discretion."

"That's Ford and Sarah Reynolds," Tomford said plainly, having witnessed it many times before.

The first time Tomford ever publicly shared his testimony, it was at a Full Gospel Businessmen's event in Gouverneur, and Ford was there. He was president of the chapter at the time. Tomford had recently graduated from college, and was thankful not only for the opportunity for God to use him in this way, but for the encouragement he received from his elder.

Ford always had a heart for the college men, wanting to see them raised up and thriving in the local church and in ministry.

"I'm sure there's people out there that don't like Ford Reynolds," Tomford tells. "But whenever I've met someone like that it was usually because they were offended by his bold witness for Jesus. But in church circles, esteem runs high for Ford and Sarah Reynolds."

Often when decisions were made in Christian Fellowship Center or Richville Christian Fellowship circles, someone would inevitably ask, "What does Ford think about this?"

After Tomford took the lead pastorate in Richville, he remembers hearing the story of Ford's faithfulness there, and that became a lesson on perseverance and an inspiration for his own journey in local church ministry. "In the years I've been at Richville, I'm consistently aware that I'm reaping where I have not sown, and a lot of that sowing was Ford and Sarah Reynolds."

Many were amazed at the grace Mike and Ford both walked in as Ford remained a member of the church long after he stepped away from the lead pastorate—and an engaged member, at that. "Not only was he around," confesses Tomford, "I wanted him around. The grace and humility he had to do that was a rare thing."

There was one demand, if not an ultimatum, that the old man had for the young pastor. "One time Ford told me," Pastor Tomford recalls, "Mike, just so you know, if you ever get rid of the mid-week prayer meeting, that's when I may have to consider going to another church."

Ford was consistent in his faith for healing. It was always on his heart, he was ready in season and out of season; he never doubted. He was always willing to give the Holy Spirit an opportunity. Even in his old age, he had a Kathryn Kuhlman book nearby, always feeding the fire of zeal and passion for miracles. "His passion has inspired me," admits Pastor Tomford. "The fact that, years later—he's 91 at the time of this interview—he's still focused on that today. He's still eager to pray for the sick. Often when I see him, one of the first things he still asks about is whether there is anyone sick so that we can pray for them.

When Tomford has been down or discouraged, his elderly friend has been there to lift up his arms, encourage him, and remind him of God's promises. He never flatters, but only points the heart back to Christ. "One thing about them," says the younger pastor of the Reynolds, "when they say they're praying for you, it's not a cliché. I know it's genuine."

God's Plan to Plant More Churches

When Lonnie Langston incorporated the church back in 1974, the founding document read *Christian Fellowship Centers,* not *Christian Fellowship Center.* The Holy Spirit deposited early in the movement a desire to plant churches. Langston had a vision of fires all over the county. Somehow, through the obedience—and weaknesses—of God's people, the vision came to pass. Many churches would grow out of the trunk of CFC—churches in Massena, Moira, Canton, Potsdam…and Richville. That would be Ford's next post after his days serving at CFC.

CHAPTER 6: PLANTING IN RICHVILLE

Ford never thought he would start a church in Richville. First of all, he was up in years. Second of all, he wasn't certain if it was his calling. But as "the wind blows where it wishes," so it seemed right to the Holy Spirit and the leaders at CFC that such a venture would be undertaken. On Sunday evening, August 30, 1992, Richville Christian Fellowship held its first service.

An old church building was vacated in the center of town, just a half mile from the farm, and Ford, along with the CFC elders, went to look at it. Not long after, they bought it for $25,000. The facility was dedicated on December 5, 1993. The first Sunday morning service was held on a stinging -40 degree morning that only northern New York knows.

The plan, when conceived, was that Rick Sinclair would be the senior pastor of the site (while continuing at CFC) and Ford would serve as a presiding elder. All that changed, however, when Sinclair sustained a head injury while playing hockey. This injury would be so debilitating that he would not be able to serve in any capacity for almost a year, and even then it would take years to be at full strength. Ford would take over all pastoral duties while continuing the work on Riverside Farm. He gradually began to sell his cows, having less and less work on the farm until May of 1997, when he would sell all the cows and retire from farming.

On October 23, 1994, an ordination service was held for Ford in the new facility to install him as the pastor of Richville Christian Fellowship. He was 67-years-old. It was a special night, marked by joyful worship, special music, fervent prayer, the fellowship of close friends and family, and a sermon from Reverend Mike Bartholomew from Watertown, New York.

Bartholomew had a tormenting sense of humor and made Ford laugh so hard, he nearly choked. He'd recounted a story from a recent trip he'd taken to Haiti where he prayed for a man named "Almighty God." Bartholomew told the translator, "Ask Almighty God what he wants." The translator inquired as to what his request might be and then answered him, "Pastor Bartholomew, Almighty God wants to be filled with the Holy Spirit!"

Ford's famous laughter filled the sanctuary.

Daughter Heidi Jo performed an original song she and her husband wrote titled "The Same Staff" for the special occasion.

Verse 1
Moses was a shepherd
For forty years was he
Many times I'm sure he'd ask
Can God still use a man like me?

And his life was growing older
But his faith was growing strong
And with the mustard seed
Deep in his heart
It wasn't long

Refrain
That with the same staff
He used to tend the flocks with
In the fields all alone
God led him down to the Land of Egypt
To lead his people home

Verse 2
Daddy was a farmer
For 50 years was he
Many times I'm sure he'd ask
Will God still use a man like me?

And his life was growing older
But his faith was growing strong
And with the mustard seed

Deep in his heart
It wasn't long

That with the same staff
He used to tend the flocks with
In the fields all alone
God led him down to the Land of Egypt
To lead his people home

Simultaneous with starting Richville Christian Fellowship, the Holy Spirit began to move on Ford's heart about increasing his time in prayer. He began by going up to the church every morning to pray for half an hour. These were solitary and precious times, and he found his love for prayer increasing, not diminishing, over time. The amount of time he prayed began to increase to around an hour, and this was an easy adjustment, as he found himself enjoying this time so much that the increase was almost unnoticed and effortless.

During this season, he also read some books on prayer by E.M. Bounds and others that inspired him greatly. One thought that stuck with him was when Bounds wrote, "Never attend a church that doesn't have a scheduled prayer meeting."

Another author wrote, "If you sense your spiritual vitality and anointing dissipating, fasting and prayer will bring it back." Ford would always strive to stay fresh, his spiritual gifts stirred up, his heart burning hot for Christ.

Some days, inspired by the testimony of a man who would do this, he would practice the principle of praying in the morning, listening, and writing down what he sensed the Holy Spirit speaking to him, and then obeying such impressions the rest of the day.

The church began with a good flock, growing to nearly 60 people within the first year. Finances would not be an issue because the overhead costs were so low, assisted further by Ford's choice to serve the church for the first eighteen months without taking a salary. Early members included St. Lawrence University professor Robert Blewett and family, a dear woman from Gouverneur named Helen Johnston (who was also Sarah's first cousin), and a handful of others. In such formative times, all hands served and made the work lighter.

Planting and growing a new church congregation was certainly a challenge. Problems developed, including a leader who would not repent of smoking marijuana. Challenges and conflicts would be frequent, just as they do in any ministry seeking to advance the gospel.

At one point, the congregation dwindled to twelve people, and Ford asked the Lord if he ought to close the doors. Planting often humbles the planters, and the Reynolds were not exceptions. People they thought would stay left just when it seemed they needed them the most, but Ford and his wife were submitted to the Hand of Providence and never grew bitter. He knew that sanctification often included lessons in humility. But how low did God want him to go? He told the Lord that he had no problem being humiliated by closing the doors if it was for His glory. He truly had the attitude, "If You're more glorified by my failure than my success, not my will but Yours be done." He just wanted his marching orders. The church continued, and not long after, had 60 people in attendance again. Had it not been for the encouragement he received in his times of prayer, the church may not exist today.

One man that attended Richville Christian Fellowship observed Ford's life of prayer and told him, "This church is here because you are a praying man."

His time in prayer convinced him, no matter what he saw outwardly, that he was in the center of God's will. He told his congregation more than once, "If I didn't think I was supposed to be here, this would be my last Sunday!"

Another testimony of the power of prayer that blessed him was of a pastor in California that felt led of the Lord to go to church every morning to pray at 6 a.m. He prayed alone for a year before the church janitor finally joined him. Others eventually came along, and the gathering grew. In the end, 600 people prayed together every morning with this young pastor. The impact was magnificent. Lost sinners were saved and many were healed.

With conviction, Ford would often say in the days that followed, "I know that if I could get 75-100 people together to pray, wonderful things would happen." Such confidence was anchored in Scripture, as such promises as are found in Luke 6:38

frequently encouraged his faith: *"Give, and it will be given to you. Good measure, pressed down, shaken together, running over, will be put into your lap. For with the measure you use it will be measured back to you"* (ESV).

The promises of Scripture for the praying man were many, and Ford gave his heart attention to them. As a farmer, another such verse that lifted his zeal to pray was, *"Do not be deceived: God is not mocked, for whatever one sows, that will he also reap. For the one who sows to his own flesh will from the flesh reap corruption, but the one who sows to the Spirit will from the Spirit reap eternal life"* (Gal. 6:7-8).

At the time of the first publication of this book, after nearly 25 years of praying, his dream of revival had still not come to pass.

Prayer would be a part of the culture at RCF in the years to come.

It must be noted that even on the hardest days in those infancy years, when the world might look and call the work a failure, God was faithful. "Low attendance never hinders what God wants to do," he would say. On a morning with only seven in attendance, an unsaved woman came forward for prayer after the message, and Ford asked her, "Do you want to be saved?"

She did.

After he prayed with her to receive Christ, he prayed for her to be healed of a progressively debilitating arthritic condition. The next morning, she knocked on the front door of the farmhouse at Riverside Farm and shared with the Reynolds that she'd been healed. "Look at my hands!" she exalted, lifting them up so they could see the radical change from the swollen, crooked version they'd seen only a day before. "They burned all night," she explained, "and when I woke up, they were healed!"

It was during these years that Charles Palmatier, a kind man and dear friend of the Reynolds family, was installed as the first elder of RCF. In later years, Alan Gratto joined the leadership as associate pastor from 2004-2008, and a good family man and man of the Word, Brian MacDonald, was set in as elder in 2008.

Also, during these early days, Ford and Sarah led a ministry to a nursing home in Gouverneur. Ford would lead a brief devotional and then pray for anyone that requested it. One elderly man told him, "I heard what you said about healing, and since the last time you were here, I haven't taken any pain medicine!" God had ministered to the old man and strengthened his body. Such reports encouraged Ford that no one was ever too old to expect the kind hand of God the Father to touch them. God regarded all of His own as children, and like any loving Father, delighted to assist them in their weakness.

Not long after, Ford began to think about having weekly healing services. Up until this point, during his days at Richville Christian Fellowship, he would simply use his healing gift in the local church services, as he visited the elderly in the nursing home ministry of the church, or as he went on visitation calls to the hospital. He would also incorporate the theme of God's power to heal the sick into his messages at RCF or wherever the pulpit was opened to him. A favorite passage was Matthew 9:18-31, a text that highlights several miracles. After the first miracle, it reads, "And the report of this went through all that district" (Matthew 8:26, ESV). After a few more verses, another miracle explodes in the narrative and gives the report, "But they went away and spread his fame through all that district" (Matthew 9:31). Ford would conclude with a pressing question: "Based on this passage, how important do you think miracles are in advancing the gospel?"

The theme of his preaching so often included healing that one woman said, "It seems you always preach on healing!"

It was his gift, his delight to see Jesus glorified in this way, and a frequent way that unbelieving eyes would be opened to who Jesus was. "Healing is what God has given me revelation on," he would say. "The message of God's power to heal was always right there in my heart." God seemed to bless the quiet and steady way his gift was infused into church life in this way, but his heart would soon be moved to be even bolder in giving God an opportunity to heal the sick.

A young man named Josh Card was showing a series of videos at Christian Fellowship Center called *God's Generals*—biographical documentaries on great divine healers. When the week came to show Kathryn Kuhlman's video, Josh invited Ford to come and testify. He was glad to do it. On the evening he went to CFC, the Lord gave him faith to start his own healing services.

It was the final nudge he needed. God had given him the gift of healing, and he knew he must steward it by giving the Holy Spirit frequent opportunities to glorify Jesus Christ.

In 1999, without any fanfare or self-aggrandizing, he put out the word that RCF would be hosting healing services. His own elder, Charlie, was a bit skeptical at first, and suggested, "At some point, Ford, you need to announce that you have the gift of healing."

"No," Ford insisted. "They'll find out in the services when God begins to move."

The services began, and so did the miracles. A woman came that had such terrible migraine headaches that she was incapacitated. She couldn't work, she couldn't run common errands, and she couldn't even manage her home. It had gotten so bad that she reversed roles with her children, and they had to take care of her. She'd been to various doctors and specialists all across New York and even down to New York City. But no one could help her. She'd visited Christian Fellowship Center several times, and found it a difficult task just to get into the building. When she finally came to Richville, she was in a desperate condition, both physically and emotionally. After Ford prayed for her, God healed her instantly. She couldn't hug him enough! In the days that followed, she didn't need medication anymore, and was able to enjoy her life and family again.

Such miracles provided God's "marketing plan" for the healing services. People began to come from far and wide. The services were never packed, but God always sent the right people, and provided answers to prayer that affirmed the gift in Ford.

One woman came who had a serious problem in her legs. She was unable to perform basic tasks like pushing a shopping cart or tending her garden without tremendous pain. Her condition was so serious and degenerative that she told Ford she could even die. The morning after he prayed for her, she called and, full of joy, reported, "I am walking and running and can do anything now!" It was miraculous. Unfortunately, this woman eventually walked away from the Lord, much like the nine lepers who were healed and did not give thanks. This would never cease to amaze Ford, how one could taste of the things of God, see his miracles, and still walk away from Him.

An 80-year-old woman named Brenda came to the church for a short time, and was then diagnosed with cancer. Her doctors told her she only had six months to live, and she decided to move to Plattsburgh with her daughter for what might be her final days. Many were praying for her. Before she left, Ford and Sarah went to her apartment in Gouverneur to pray for her. Her belly looked like that of a pregnant woman, as the tumor inside had become enormous. They prayed for her and not long after that time, she moved, as planned, to Plattsburgh. The Reynolds eventually lost touch with her.

A few years later, Ford and Sarah went to a local nursing home to sing some hymns, and Brenda's sister was there. They inquired about their old friend and she said, "She doesn't have cancer anymore!"

"Really?!" Ford responded with delighted laughter.

This made them curious, so they decided to drive to Plattsburgh to see Brenda. When they arrived, her hair was all fixed up, and she was truly a beautiful elderly woman with the light of Christ on her countenance. They confirmed with their own eyes what they had heard—that she was cancer-free! Once again this affirmed to Ford and Sarah that their heavenly Father saw all of those who followed Him, no matter their age, as His little children. There is no age when He would be unwilling to grant a healing. He cares for all His children—even His old ones. Just as the Bible says, "As a father shows compassion to his children, so the Lord shows compassion to those who fear him."

In the end, Brenda lived eight more years after Ford and Sarah had prayed for her. And she did not die of cancer.

The local newspaper published an article about the story of Richville Christian Fellowship, and Ford said about this time, "We have seen many wonderful manifestations of God's healing power through the years. These meetings continue today."

Not only did Ford minister at RCF, but continued to sow into the congregation at CFC from time to time.

He went to minister at a mid-week gathering and prayed for the sick. One woman came forward and, though she did not express precisely what her need was, Ford prayed for her. As the service ended, she remained standing in the front. Ford later found out that she couldn't move. She was entranced at the altar.

Eventually, the church workers had to turn off the lights and lock up the building. As the woman still couldn't move, some church members carried her out, took her home, and helped her into her house. After she got inside, she discovered that one of her legs, significantly shorter than the other, requiring a lift on one of her shoes, had grown out and her legs were even.

Ford heard the story and rejoiced. Surely there were doubters, but, Ford reasoned, could not a God who said "let there be" and "there was" to creation, speak a word that might extend a woman's leg? That would be a small thing for a mighty God to do.

On another occasion, a deaf young woman attending one of the local colleges came to one of the healing services, and when Ford prayed for her, she exclaimed, "I can hear! I can hear!"

Testimonies like these surely encouraged the saints and emboldened them to pray for others.

Of course, as any sower, Ford always hoped to see more miracles and more answer to prayer. He was never unamazed at miracles, but also found himself befuddled at times when someone wasn't healed. When asked why, sometimes he would have no more answers than the one asking the question. He knew God could do anything and he knew he had a gift from the Lord, but as to why God would heal sometimes and not others was puzzling. He attributed it to God's sovereignty and never allowed such musings to stop his next prayer. "You can't figure God out!" he would say. "God is God and you have to let Him be God. We have to praise God for whatever He does and whatever He doesn't do."

More Miracles

One Easter Sunday morning, Ford preached on resurrection power. At the end of the message, he boldly welcomed anyone that had a "dead" part of their body to present themselves to the Lord in faith, that they might experience the resurrection power of Jesus. One woman had lifted her withered hand before the Lord during the meeting. Like the man in the gospel story, she was ashamed of her withered hand, and would normally cover it so others couldn't see it. To lift it up before the Lord was not only an act of faith, but an act of humility. Nothing happened that morning, and nothing was reported to Ford even about the fact that the woman had prayed for healing. The next day, the woman took a nap, and when she woke, her hand was completely whole! When news reached Ford's ears, he rejoiced at the goodness of God.

The testimony of her hand being healed while she slept also presented a suitable picture of the gospel itself, as the Savior calls sinners to Himself while they slumber in sin. We as a human race were lost in apathy, ignorance, and naiveté to God; any surfacing emotion toward Him was hostility or skepticism. We were sleeping in a wretched spiritual state. But the Father, rich in mercy and grace, invaded us, broke into our world against our will, rescuing us from sin and brokenness that might have otherwise overtaken us. Such gospel concepts drove Ford to preach and to pray, a partaker of such sweet grace himself.

A woman named Ginny Palmatier who had been a part of RCF for many years developed Stage 4 ovarian cancer. The prognosis was grim. She went to a hospital in Syracuse, New York, for evaluation and treatment, and Ford made the two-hour journey south to visit her and pray with her. The cancer disappeared! Six years later, she was diagnosed with lung cancer. Ford and the church prayed for her again, and again the cancer disappeared. Why did the cancer return? Ford was well aware that as long as we are in this fallen world, we will find ourselves dealing with the effect of its fallen state, including its effect on our bodies. This may mean multiple battles with sin or sickness. One, therefore, ought to walk in prayer as often as we are confronted by such a depraved world, which is, of course, continuously.

As they continued hosting healing services in Richville and God continued to be generous, Ford shared with Rick Sinclair about what God was doing, and soon they planned some healing meetings at Christian Fellowship Center. Stories of divine healing abounded from these gatherings as well.

Ford was convinced that God simply needed an opportunity. If you give Him one, he believed, He would be faithful.

At CFC, one boy was healed of a recessed testicle. His mother had been praying for some time, and when Ford prayed for him, the testicle dropped. The mother was extremely grateful to Ford and the Lord. (As was the boy, one might be sure.)

On the same night, Ford prayed for a certain red-haired woman who wore a long dress, and he had the keen sense that God wanted to do a great miracle for her. He told her, "I just believe God wants to give you a miracle."

With that, he prayed for the woman. She seemed to be entranced for hours. In the days that followed, Ford was informed that this woman was actually a man that had, for years, been tormented by gender confusion, fear and depression. He had lived with all the lights on in his house every day, 24 hours a day. He finally made the decision to get a sex change, but even in that, could not escape the mental anguish that had plagued him for so long. Visits to the church were often interrupted by anxiety attacks, and he'd have to leave during the services. But something happened the night Ford prayed for him. By a work of grace through the Holy Spirit, the bondages were broken, and he was free! He explained that the Spirit of God had freed him, like chains had been broken off, from the fear and anxiety that had gripped him for so long. He would continue life as a man, submitting his sexuality to Christ, and eventually found himself serving in ministry for many years.

After a season, the healing services at CFC ended, but the deposit in the hearts of God's people would abide. Not only had Ford exercised his gift, but had stirred such a gift in the hearts of many, young and old, to trust the good heart and strong arm of God to heal again.

In the years that followed, Ford would go to minister at Christian Fellowship Center when invited. In 2009, he taught on the gift of healing in Sunday School classes and then spoke in the main service on God's sovereignty. Just as 1 John 2:13-14 says, fathers "know him who is from the beginning." So it was with Ford. After so many years of walking with the Lord, he could see the Hand of Providence working in all things, the Alpha and the Omega; the One who knew the end from the beginning. His desire was to show his hearers a God who reigned and was worthy of their trust, even when answers to questions or prayers were delayed, or trials lingered.

Conversions

There was a woman who had received Christ at a healing service who brought her unsaved brother to Richville Christian Fellowship. After the service, he went to Ford with tears in his eyes and asked him, "Will you go and see my brother?"

His brother was very sick, and knew nothing of salvation by grace.

Moved by this man's faith, Ford went immediately. After sharing the good news of salvation with the ailing brother, any resistance the man might have had withered in the light of God's love, and he repented of his sins and placed his faith in the Lord Jesus. Afterward he had such a dramatic change in his physical condition that he didn't even need to take his pain medication anymore. His brother marveled at the power of God and praised Him for His amazing grace.

Church Planting

Planting a church was not all glorious stories of salvations, signs, and wonders. Ford and Sarah both learned it was neither for the faint of heart nor for those who didn't want to get their hands dirty. Admittedly not good at delegating anyway, they found themselves both carrying a lot of the weight of the work of the church. Ford not only carried the ministerial duties, but menial tasks abounded. He mowed the yard, managed the building, often opened up, set up, and locked up. He even had to try to engineer a barely functional sound system. Eventually, he worked with his son-in-law to design a simple, state-of-the-art system suitable to their needs.

Sarah's work abounded as well, but her work might be better seen and appreciated in the context of their marriage.

Their Marriage

An old saying says, "Marital love is like fine wine—it gets better with time." So it was with the Reynolds. As the years went on, and the journey of faith, family, and ministry continued, Ford found his heart full when his wife was at his side. All he had known from his friend and partner was support and encouragement. She never held him back, but saw the gift, encouraged the gift, and released the gift. She never doubted her husband when he found his heart convinced of something God had called him to, but followed him with a whole heart. She was honest, but did not whine or nag; strong, but not antagonistic or rebellious; concerned, but never a slave to fear or hesitation.

She was a true "completer"; a true partner in ministry. She remembered things he would forget, and more than anything, did not feel she needed recognition or position outside the home to validate herself or raise her importance. Raising the children and serving her husband filled her heart with joy, and never left her without work! Even so, she was not afraid to serve needs outside the home just as is fitting for a Proverbs 31 woman, but saw it as her duty to bless others through her home. As the kids got older and moved out, she found herself far more able to give time to the church. During the season of planting and growing RCF, she gave much of her time to the work, carrying administrative weight at times while mobilizing other women to serve in hospitality, and keeping the church facility tidy. Much of her contribution was doing the little things in the back of the church that few would volunteer to do: cleaning, cooking, preparing coffee, and other menial tasks that were important to the work of Christian community.

At other times, she was the voice God would use to encourage her husband when physical or spiritual weariness would come after a barrage of demand. She would comfort, but also motivated her man to endure in the work of the Lord, that he might fulfill a duty, meet a need, or simply attend a gathering.

While excelling as a wife, Sarah was not a novice with the Scriptures. Exposed to the Bible since she was a child, she could encourage, counsel, exhort, and if necessary, correct. This is not to say she would impose herself, but she was a capable co-laborer in the gospel. As she ministered to others, it was always in a nurturing, caring, tender, motherly way befitting of a godly woman. Those who received from her care would know comfort and strength.

To contrast, her husband did not have the Scripture-centric background that she'd known. Converted at 42, he was a perpetual learner, though sometimes felt himself inferior to his wife when it came to Scriptural knowledge. Her husband was bold and zealous, but many times she worried about what he might say when he spoke, knowing his ministerial life was one of learning on the job. If she found an error, she would lovingly caution her Apollos, and imitate earlier saints who "took him and explained to him the way of God more accurately" (Acts 18:26).

Other times, Ford would be careless, mentioning names of people he ought not in a public presentation. Again, his Priscilla would lovingly and gently correct him.

He would unashamedly testify, "If I wasn't listening to the Holy Spirit, I would then hear from God through my wife!" When God's voice was quiet, hers was loud and clear!

He would often tell the congregation that without his beloved wife, he couldn't do it.

On Being a Pastor

The same thing that brought so much blessing and joy to being a pastor was often the same thing that made it so difficult: people. Moses, weary of an entire career of dealing with complainers, struck a rock in anger. Even Jesus found his humanity stretched to its limit, it would seem, when he saw the carnality of his disciples and said, "How long shall I put up with you?"

Ford learned to expect criticism and take his blows in stride. He always tried to see another's perspective, and when he found himself dealing with an unreasonable person, looked upward. As one might expect in any church, he dealt with immaturity and ignorance, divisions and factions, immorality and offenses. He knew that, just as Jesus taught, “the poor you will always have with you.” Some demanded to preach; others demanded a church after their own image. In one man's exit interview from the church, he told Ford, "The problem is that we often left the Sunday services feeling guilty." Such criticism was likely to encourage Ford rather than discourage him, as he always welcomed the conviction of the Holy Spirit. At the same time, he was left to wonder at men like this, because his ultimate desire was not only that they would be convicted, but forgiven and free. Guilt was not the destination of his preaching. Grace was.

Ford would seek to be the first to resolve a conflict, and was, by grace, self-aware of his own weaknesses and faults, willing to own his contribution to any tension. The ups and downs would come and go. A combination of immature people, deceived people, and the devil would make his battles plenty, though he's always been known to say, "If you never run into the devil, you're going the wrong direction."

Such battles reinforced what he already knew: That he was not to find his identity in the fickleness of men's praises, in his position, or others' opinions of him. His confidence and security must be in the Lord, for that is the only place for a pastor to stand.

Among the challenges, God was faithful to our friend and the work at RCF. Many had heard the gospel and many were saved. Many miracles were wrought and Jesus was being glorified. This was all that mattered to him.

In the midst of it all, the seasoned couple found sanctifying grace for them and their congregation. They learned to lean more on the Spirit and trust the will of their Father. Elisabeth Elliot once said, and the Reynolds found it to be true, that *"God will see to it that we are in circumstances best designed by His sovereign love to give us opportunities to bear fruit for Him."*

God was also faithful to send along faithful and loyal men who would stand with the Reynolds and with the church. Such a man was the aforementioned Charlie Palmatier, a tender-hearted man who loved his family in Christ with great joy and affection. He was well-known in the community as he, at one time, had been the music director at Gouverneur High School. He seemed to have the gift of laughter, and the gift to make others laugh, believing the Bible to be true when it said, "A joyful heart is good medicine, but a crushed spirit dries up the bones" (Proverbs 17:22). He was an encourager to Ford and to many in RCF, but was also strong when he needed to be. If one would come to criticize his leader, Palmatier would say, "I come here because Ford lives what he preaches." Ford was able to lean on such a man at times, and share the weight of the ministry with him. He counted him a friend, and when Palmatier died in September of 2002, his loss was a painful one for Ford and for the small church in northern New York.

Ozreal

A kind man named Ozreal joined the church along with his wife, Loretta. They were Jamaican immigrant farmers, and had a sweet and sincere faith that blessed the congregation at RCF. They were loyal and faithful to the point that one might call their steadiness a gift, attending services every time the doors were open—rain, snow, or shine. In Ford's words, "They were regular as clockwork." Ozreal was also a generous man, frequently giving vegetables from his own garden to anyone that might have need.

After several years, this dear servant of the Lord was afflicted with throat cancer. The prognosis was not hopeful. Doctors didn't give him long to live.

Ford was always careful not to presume to know what God's will might be, but in this instance it would be different. One morning, as he prayed for Ozreal, the Holy Spirit spoke to his heart, "This sickness is not unto death."

One Sunday during the service, Ford and the elders prayed for him with the laying on of hands. The congregation joined them, and soon he was treated. The cancer completely disappeared.

When Ozreal's wife Loretta told Ford that the cancer was gone, Ford asked her, "Where did it go, Loretta?"

She was overwhelmed with joy. "The Lord took it!"

For a whole year, Ozreal was completely whole. But then the cancer returned to his throat, this time to a different place.

Ozreal grew worse and worse, and Ford pleaded with the Lord again, that death might not take him. "Lord," he prayed, "you said that this sickness was not unto death!"

But as he prayed, the Lord showed him that he indeed had healed him the first time, but that this was a new sickness. This would be the final battle of Ozreal's life, as he went to be with the Lord not many days after.

Such an experience taught Ford not to speak where God might be silent. God's spirit had spoken a promise the first time, but not the second. Just as Hezekiah "became sick and was at the point of death" (Isaiah 38:1, ESV) and the Lord spared him, granting him fifteen more years, so the Lord had interceded for Ozreal, mercifully adding two years to his life, but had also appointed his days.

Though puzzling, Ford learned to submit humbly to the will of God in such matters, content to suspend judgment and avoid demanding answers. The morning light of eternity would make all things bright and clear, he believed, though now we see dimly.

Reputation in Richville

In 2003, Ford was asked to preach in the United Church of Richville. When someone called to invite him, he said, "Are you sure?"

The woman, representing the prudential committee, answered, "You're very respected in this town!"

It would be his first visit in years.

How things had changed in a few decades. The one that was counted among the fanatics was now being esteemed and invited back to a place he was persecuted. This was both redemptive and vindicating. It was not his own glory he sought, mind you, but the glory of God, and he saw this invitation as something that exalted his heavenly Father and restored unity.

Just as the seasons can change abruptly in northern New York from the beauty of fall to the harshness of winter or to the rains of spring to the lazy days of summer, so Ford and Sarah's life was changing. They would soon step away from leading the ministry at Richville Christian Fellowship.

CHAPTER 7: SOWING AND REAPING

In 2004, Ford's daughter Heidi Jo was going through the Canadian border in Ogdensburg, reentering the United States with her husband Derek. "Where are you going?" the border patrol officer asked the couple, stern and serious.

"Richville," answered Derek.

"Where in Richville?" the officer politely demanded.

"We're going to her parents' farm, the Reynolds' place on Route 11."

The officer leaned down into the window and peered at Heidi Jo in the passenger seat. "You're Ford Reynolds' daughter?" he asked, his countenance and mood suddenly lightening.

"Yes I am," she answered.

The officer straightened up and motioned forward. "Go on through. Have a nice day."

Ford was a known and esteemed man. His reputation as a man of integrity could expedite his daughter's family through an international border.

In November of 2008, the same month Barack Obama was elected president, a special celebration was held for Ford's 80th birthday. It was attended by many from CFC and RCF, along with his immediate and extended family. It was a blessed time, where many publicly testified of how the Reynolds had blessed their lives. Further, many eyes could see the fruit of the life of a couple who had obeyed and walked with the Lord. Their children "rose up and called them blessed" and their grandchildren sat at their feet.

This time not only encouraged the old couple, but blessed the many who came and marveled at the goodness of God. Even some in the extended family, who once thought Ford and Sarah to be extreme or had previously been skeptical, had a change of heart when they saw the blessing of God in the lives of these aging gospel warriors. "You're a VIP!" one of Ford's elderly sisters exclaimed. His relationships with his entire extended family, though once facing colder days, were all healthy and strong.

Within the following year, a younger leader named Michael Tomford came to lead the work in Richville. A kind man, a family man, he had been on staff for years as an assistant at Christian Fellowship Center, and now came the call to labor in the rural harvest fields of southern St. Lawrence County. The new pastor had known Ford Reynolds for a long time and held him in highest esteem.

On February 1, 2009, a few months after he turned 81-years-old, Ford retired from being lead pastor of Richville Christian Fellowship, though he would continue as an elder. On one hand, he and Sarah would miss being as deeply involved in the work of the ministry as they had been. On the other hand, they were now able to sow freely in the Body of Christ locally and wherever God might open the door for them to do so.

One of those doors came through the plea of an old acquaintance, who requested prayer as he was dying of liver failure. Ford opened to John Chapter 3 and told him, "Jesus said that you must be born again."

"I was in church for eleven years," the man said, "and nobody ever told me that I needed to be born again!"

Ford prayed with the man to receive Christ.

No matter how many times he prayed for someone to be delivered from a sickness, an injury, or some other besetting crisis, he was always convinced that the greatest miracle was salvation. He rejoiced greatly whenever someone would repent of their sins and put their faith in Jesus, and he counted it the most wonderful miracle of all!

Ford felt strongly about the need for a gospel preacher to proclaim, "You must be born again!" He was convicted that we must say what Jesus said. This is precisely what Kathryn Kuhlman proclaimed on street corners when she was 16-years-old. One might not wonder why his feelings were so strong about this when one of the main instruments God used to bring him to Christ preached the born again gospel with such conviction.

Further, it was what his own wife told him before his conversion! How could he accept any other message?

Ford continued to pray for the sick at RCF any time such a need arose, and though his physical strength might wane, the gift did not. His spiritual strength was fresh and strong in Christ.

He was invited to come and minister downstate in Gallupville, New York, a small town to the west of Albany. A Pentecostal pastor named Jim Wolford invited him. Wolford, though young enough to be his son, made a connection with Ford not only as a co-laboring worker in God's harvest fields, but also as a one-time farmer in nature's cornfields. Ford's pastoral ministry began after he retired from farming at age 67. Jim's ministry began at age 19 after he grew up on a farm.

Saved in 1974, God called Wolford in 1978 to lay down the dream of running his own farm and plant a church in the small town of Gallupville, population 800 (at the time). Ford's son-in-law, the author of this book, would get saved as a boy in this new church. This biography, in fact, is in the reader's hands today because of Jim Wolford's obedience to start Gallupville Gospel Church.

Ford saw two miracles when he ministered at Gallupville. Just like the evangelist is satisfied if God reaches one, so a minister with the gift of healing is satisfied to see even one healed. The fact that he saw two miracles, however, is notable, as Wolford had, not long before Ford came, brought in an evangelist who had traveled the world and seen many miracles in the nations, but none in Gallupville.

Everywhere Ford went, on first visits especially, the Holy Spirit would move in signs and wonders, but more often than not, he wouldn't be invited back. This baffled him. He never grew bitter over it, but was left to wonder why, even when there was fruit, that some churches were not interested in continuing to experience such wonderful things. He never asked to go anywhere or hassled pastors to open their doors to him. He would only go where he was invited.

No matter where he went, opportunities were never more prevalent than right in his own community. A woman named Shirley Fenlong, who had been part of Richville Christian Fellowship, had been suffering with severe back problems. This affliction made it difficult to work and perform even the most basic, ordinary tasks. She heard Ford preach one morning at RCF when Tomford was away, and she was the only one who came up for prayer. Ford laid hands on her in prayer and asked God to heal her. After she went home from the service, she called him right away, rejoicing that she'd been healed of her affliction.

Later on, this same woman had "fibroid tumors" and the accompanying painful cramps in her abdomen. She called Ford and asked for prayer, which he obliged, but afterward the pain got worse! She called a second time and said in jest, "I don't ever want you to pray for me again!" However, not long after, she had a checkup and the tumors had disappeared.

In late 2009, he was asked to come and teach on healing at New Testament Church in Massena, New York. As was his way, he prayed for anyone that wanted prayer after his message. A young woman asked for deliverance from her addiction to cigarette smoking. Months later, when Ford came to Massena again, she ran across the sanctuary and proclaimed with a big smile, "I haven't had a cigarette since the night you prayed for me!"

Right around this time, Ford was invited to be part of a healing team at Koinonia for some special services. A lawyer named Vern Ingram said, "I heard you have a healing ministry? I wonder if you'd be willing to come over and join us for some special gatherings?" Ford prayed for a woman who was suffering from a disease in one of her eyes and was nearly blind. The next morning after Ford prayed for her, she called and said, "You seem to be the leader of the healing team. I'd want you to know that I can see out of that eye now well enough to drive!"

There have been three times when those with afflictions in the eyes have testified of receiving a drastic improvement in their vision, though never 100% (perhaps now and not yet??). Ford couldn't explain that, but was thankful for any blessing the Lord would give to these mortal, temporal, and often broken bodies. At these same meetings, there was a young woman in college that had an affliction in her legs that made them so weak that she couldn't even climb stairs. It forced her to alter her life so much that she had to get a first-floor apartment. God gave Ford much faith for this woman and he looked her right in the eyes and said,

"Are you ready to get healed?" She went outside and began running around the church. One of the other pastors in attendance marveled at this and praised God. Within a few weeks, Ford received a letter from Vern Ingram, who told Ford that this young woman's legs were strong enough to climb stairs.

Over the years he prayed for many people, and he knew that God would always do some things he would never hear about. Other miracles were gradual, and he would hear at a later time, or perhaps the person wouldn't credit God for the healing. Remember, however, Ford never stopped being convinced that God is as good at slow miracles as He is at fast ones. Is it any less a miracle if the Lord heals gradually than if He heals instantly? All power of life is in God's hands, the Author of Life. Jesus turned water into wine—a miracle that happens every day in nature, but when Jesus sped it up at the wedding of Cana, people marveled.

Ministering and sowing seeds for so many years, Ford and Sarah began to see this verse become a reality in their lives: "Cast your bread upon the waters, for you will find it after many days" (Ecclesiastes 11:1, ESV). They had sown much, and were reaping much. It was not uncommon for a person to re-emerge from days past and testify of how their ministry had impacted them.

One day, Ford attended a wake and was approached by someone he didn't even recognize. "Years ago, you prayed for me," explained the man, "and I've never been the same since!"

Such encouragement would inspire faith in Ford and Sarah to continue sowing! "I guess God knows that we all need encouragement once in a while," Ford would say. "He's faithful to let us see, every so often, how a seed has grown!"

In the fall of 2011, he was invited to a local church in Norfolk, New York, led by friend Bill Huckle. Bill was a man who loved the Lord deeply, and longed for revival. He always sought to create opportunities for the Holy Spirit to move in the lives of his congregation and in his community, and so he invited Ford to minister at some healing services. People brought their sick and afflicted, and Ford prayed over them. A certain woman came up for prayer, and Ford felt led to "plead the blood of Jesus" over her problem, whatever it was. When the woman returned to her seat, blood flowed out of her wrist and ran down her arm. It was enough to soak a tissue. She immediately realized that she was healed of her affliction. Though she didn't tell Ford what she was healed of, the flowing blood was surely a strange "sign and wonder" of a supernatural work.

"The thing about signs and wonders," Ford would say, "is that they make you wonder!" Huckle would tell Ford many days later that the woman had a red spot on her wrist ever since that evening.

The same night this happened, another woman that had been suffering with great pain from three herniated discs was healed on her way to the service. She had seen advertisements in the newspaper for the healing services and she decided to attend. God met her before she even arrived. This was a mark of the reality of grace in divine healing and in salvation itself. Before the woman did anything that one might think warrants a healing, the strong arm of the Lord reached out to her. Grace. What had she done to attain such a miracle? Nothing, save having her vehicle pointed toward Christ. Likewise, Jesus often finds a man or woman before they find Him. To demonstrate the unmerited favor and the gift that salvation is, He may catch a sinner by surprise. Paul the Apostle knew something of this grace, as, while his feet walked toward Damascus to persecute Jesus, the One he sought to afflict afflicted him with such grace and love that he would never be the same. This miracle also proved that Ford Reynolds is not the healer, Jesus is.

He rejoiced at the report of the woman's miracle. She never had pain from that affliction again. It might be worthy of note to remember that such a miracle also occurred in Kathryn Kuhlman's ministry. To whatever degree it might be properly concluded, God had repeated the genre of miracle in the student that he had once given the teacher. Not that Kuhlman and Ford had any direct mentoring relationship, but her ministry was certainly used to train up this farmer-healer from the North Country.

In 2014, Ford's grandson Jack faced a painful and dangerous situation when the 3-year-old's appendix burst. "Please take me to the hospital!" the little boy cried out to his mother Heidi Jo in agony. If there was any question before then about how serious the child's affliction was, all doubt disappeared. Rushed to the hospital, the boy was immediately examined by medical staff and the family was informed of their son's condition. Emergency surgery would be required.

Heidi called her father and he prayed with such passion and faith that she could feel it through the phone. All went well and the boy fully recovered, and quite quickly, at that.

One early morning in May of 2018, the phone rang at 5 a.m. It was a close friend whose husband had a brain hemorrhage and he was on a ventilator in Gouverneur. The situation looked bleak. He needed to be transported to the hospital in Syracuse, but due to a storm, all life flights were grounded. To make matters worse, there wasn't even a certified ambulance (for someone in his condition) available to take him. Sarah listened as her friend talked about the agony of waiting all night, wondering if her husband would die. "I just wanted to hear your voice," she told her friend.

Sarah woke up her husband, and they prayed over the phone for a miracle. Afterward, they went right to the hospital to pray over the suffering man in person. Seeing the condition he was in, they knew it would take a miracle to save him. Even after he finally made it to Syracuse, the surgeon concluded that his case was hopeless. In spite of the discouraging report, the family decided to operate, wanting to give every possible chance for their loved one to be healed. Against all odds, the surgery was successful and he lives to this day.

"We pray for people," Ford would say afterward, "but it's up to God what happens, and how it happens! It wouldn't have given ten cents for his life when I saw him. That was a tremendous miracle!"

"I'm glad you were there," the man's wife told him.

He smiled and laughed his famous laughter. "I'm glad God was there!"

In recent years, Ford has noticed a greater hesitation in the Body of Christ for people to ask God for healing and to come forward during church services to receive prayer for healing. This has, in his estimation, resulted in fewer miracles. He longs for pastors and preachers to create an environment of expectation and faith, so God's children can freely receive their inheritance in

Christ, part of which is healing, as the Psalmist said, "Forget not all His benefits...who heals all your diseases."[2]

His passion for prayer has continued to increase with his age. It would be a regular part of his private life, and he would always be seeking to gather the saints corporately.

Healing was something that God embedded in his spirit from the day he met Christ. He just knew deep in his heart that there was no disease God could not heal, and wouldn't heal. He was convinced that God could even raise the dead.

In a sense, that's exactly what God did with this farmer-evangelist-pastor-healer-son who was once a slave to dead religion. How could he ever doubt the resurrection power of a Savior that raised such a dead heart from the state it had been in? He knew, because of his own conversion, that wherever the gospel is preached, they shall be healed.

The days ahead, and perhaps eternity, alone will show the glorious outcome of a lifetime of sowing and reaping in God's kingdom. "Therefore, my beloved brothers, be steadfast, immovable, always abounding in the work of the Lord, knowing that in the Lord your labor is not in vain" (1 Corinthians 15:58, ESV). Seeds sown in faith will reap a glorious harvest. The gospel made its way to Ford Reynolds. Then it made its way through Ford Reynolds. Where will it go from here?

---

[2] Psalm 103:3

CHAPTER 8: QUESTIONS AND ANSWERS

There are many questions today surrounding the topic of divine healing, and though Ford concedes that he doesn't own all the answers, his reflections based on years of experience might prove profitable. The following are his own answers to common questions about divine healing.

Is it God's will to heal every time?

Ford: The Bible does not differentiate between who God will heal and who He won't. It doesn't say that He'll heal everybody but this one. It doesn't say "everybody except." It says He bore our sicknesses—everybody's sicknesses!—on the tree. I preach that healing is for everybody. When I pray for someone, I have no reason to think otherwise— especially as I read passages like Psalm 103—than the fact that God can heal them and *wants* to heal them except for where I see Paul's thorn in the flesh. He wasn't set free from that. I've heard preachers use that as an example that it's not God's will to heal every time, but where the Bible instructs us to lay hands on the sick, it doesn't give a disclaimer that we should only lay hands on some sick. You can't say that it's for *certain* people, because if you do, people with weak faith will always assume they are the ones disqualified. Everyone must come with faith. How come some don't get healed? I don't know why that is. And I don't mind telling people. I don't have the answers to those things. But I'm not going to preach that it's not for everybody because that's just not what the Bible says. Jesus never turned anybody down. Even the Syrophoenician woman was received and healed by Him.

We have to preach the Word. If He says it's for everybody, then it's for everybody. Then we leave the results up to Him. Sometimes healing is later in heaven, but many times it's *now*. Jesus has *now power*.

From the author: We also need to understand the "now and not yet" of our salvation. The Bible teaches that we *are* saved (2 Timothy 1:9), we *are being* saved (1 Corinthians 1:18; 15:2), and we *shall be* saved (Romans 5:9-10). This reminds us that though we can confidently say we are saved *now*, there is also a sense in which our salvation is a future event. So now we live in the in-betweens, the now and not yet. Healing might be seen in the same light. There is a sense in which we are healed *now*, and the Christian should have faith that God can heal now, but even the greatest miracle that's ever happened to a person's physical state has withered away and their life ended in death. So our ultimate, final healing lies before us as a future event. What I am saying is that we need to allow God to be God in our pursuit of divine healing, as some healing is *now*, and some *not yet*. The degree to which we all experience that is up to Him.

Why does God heal some and not others?

Ford: As I've said, I don't know. There are some things that make a difference though, and faith is one of them. We see in Jesus' hometown that unbelief was definitely a hindrance.

What has to happen, in your understanding, for a person to receive a healing?

Ford: The gift of faith enters in. The gift of healing enters in. Those are probably the two main gifts that must be present. The faith of the person that comes to me contributes in some way, just as Jesus would often say, "Your faith has made you whole."

By the gift of faith, I mean that sometimes I personally have supernatural faith that the person is going to be healed. Sometimes I'm just convinced that it's the will of God, and I pray with that confidence.

By the gift of healing, I mean the literal gift of God working through a person to heal. I have no healing power on my own, but God, at His desire, supernaturally uses me as an instrument to see people healed. I'm totally dependent upon God. I can't heal anyone. When God does and doesn't I can't figure out, but I know it's not about how perfect my prayer is or how loud I pray. God heals at His desire. I've simply learned to obey and pray. Because I know that this gift is at work in my life, I expect this gift to work as He sees fit.

These two often work together, though I have seen God heal people without me sensing a great measure of faith in myself. Even so, because I've seen God heal so many people, I find it easier to have faith when I pray. He's done it before, and I know He can and will do it again. So these gifts seems to build up each other.

When do you rebuke the spirit of infirmity and when do you pray for healing?

Ford: Most of the time I just pray for the sick. Sometimes, if there's an obvious demonic element active in the person, I'll take authority over it. If a person in this condition gets delivered from demonic oppression, they're usually healed. Sometimes you see Jesus doing this, like in the story of the Gadarene demoniac in Luke 8:26-39 and or the boy in Luke 9:37-43. But even with Jesus himself, the little boy threw himself on the ground and resisted. I've seen some pretty dramatic manifestations like this, and yet, other times, I've seen people with demonic oppression show little reaction at all.

Can all believers be used in healing ministry, and do you think it's God's will that all believers be used in healing ministry?

Ford: Mark 16:17-18 says, "And these signs will accompany those who believe: in my name they will cast out demons...they will lay their hands on the sick, and they will recover." All that believe are qualified to lay hands on the sick. All believers can heal the sick.

The difference between one with the gift of healing and one without it is simply how often it happens. To be sure, every time God heals it's a gift of healing, but a person with the gift of healing usually has more faith than someone that doesn't have the gift, and sees more miracles happen. The gift of faith is the same way. Whenever someone has faith for healing, they have received a gift of faith, but the gift of faith is marked by consistency, not only for one's own healing, but for others as well.

What would you say to those who do not believe that the gifts are for today?

Ford: I guess I'd have to tell them what I've seen! If they aren't for today, then who's performing these miracles that are glorifying Jesus? The Scriptures don't say it was just for yesteryear. The Bible says that Jesus is the same yesterday, today, and forever! And if He's still alive—and of course, we know that He is—then He's still doing the same things yesterday, today, and forever.

How important are miracles in the Church today?

Ford: Well, in John 14, Jesus said, "Believe me because of the works I do." When John the Baptist sent his disciples to Jesus to ask if he was the One in Luke 7, Jesus said to them, "Go and tell John what you have seen and heard: the blind receive their sight, the lame walk, lepers are cleansed, and the deaf hear, the dead are raised up, the poor have good news preached to them." So Jesus was pointing directly to his miracles as a sign of who He was. So, I believe it's very important!

Do we need miracles today? Yes! In John 14, Jesus said that his followers would do greater works. We need to trust God to use us to see those works. People still today will flock to healing services where people are getting healed. They might not get saved, but they'll come hear the message!

What would you say to someone who struggles with doubt?

Ford: Faith comes by hearing and hearing by the word of God. If they have doubts, they need to hear the message over and over again. Kenneth Hagin was on his bed at 15 years of age and he was pretty much an invalid. He read Mark 11:24, where it says, "Therefore I tell you, whatever you ask in prayer, believe that you have received it, and it will be yours" (ESV). He read it over and over and over again. Finally, one morning, it became life to him and he was totally healed. He got out of his bed, and much to the astonishment of his family, went down to breakfast. Hagin preached until he was 86-years-old.

So hearing the word and meditating on it until it is internalized will help the doubter. I tell people, "The more you're in church, the more faith you'll have. You need to be in church and hear the Word!" That's what the Bible teaches! Some people say, "I don't need to go to church. I'm saved." Yes, you do! You need to constantly position yourself to hear the Word of God. If you can't go to church, bring the church to you. No one has an excuse.

Finally, my relationship with the Lord has been enhanced because of my prayer life. God is real to me—a lot more so than He was before my prayer time. This strikes a great blow to my doubts. If God is real to me, I've got more faith! I *know* God is hearing my prayer.

James 1:6-7 says, "But let him ask in faith, with no doubting, for the one who doubts is like a wave of the sea that is driven and tossed by the wind. For that person must not suppose that he will receive anything from the Lord." So without faith it's impossible to please God, and since faith comes by hearing, we need to hear! We have to grow out of our doubts by constantly exposing ourselves to God's Word.

WEDDING DAY, SEPTEMBER 29, 1962

FAMILY PORTRAIT, CIRCA 1980 (COUNTER-CLOCKWISE: FORD, SARAH, HEIDI, JILL, LAURIE, JAMIE)

PRAYER OVER FORD & SARAH AT RICHVILLE CHRISTIAN FELLOWSHIP IN 2021.

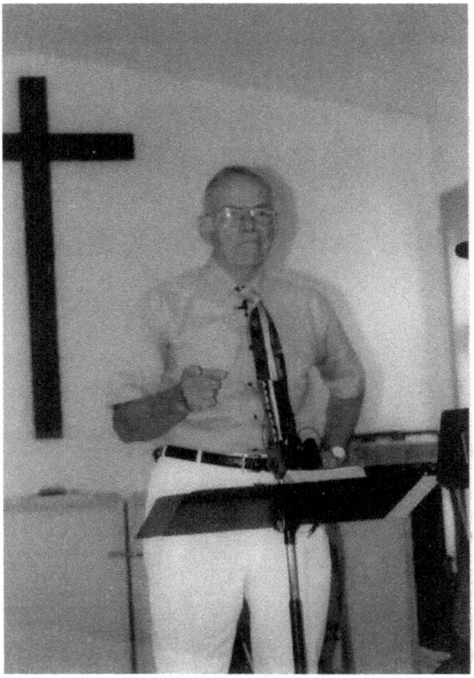

FORD REYNOLDS CIRCA 2019

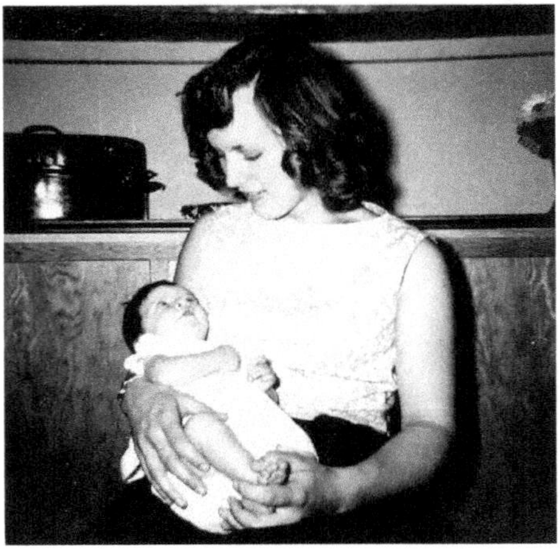

SARAH AND BABY LAURIE (FIRSTBORN) IN 1963

FORD REYNOLDS IN 2021 (PHOTO: CONNIE HARTLE)